Which seeds shall grow?

To Pauline,

with best wishes,

Naomi.

271.2
TUR

Which seeds shall grow?

MEN AND WOMEN
IN RELIGIOUS LIFE

Naomi Turner

Collins Dove

Published by COLLINS DOVE
60-64 Railway Road, Blackburn, Victoria 3130

Cover design by Mary Goodburn
Cover illustration by Susan Daily
Designed by Jo Brazil
Typeset in $1\frac{1}{12}$ Vladimir by Solo
Printed in Australia by The Book Printer

National Library of Australia
Cataloguing-in-Publication data:

Turner, Naomi.
    Which seeds shall grow?
    ISBN 0 85924 704 X

    1. Nuns – Australia – Interviews. 2. Brothers (in
    religious orders, congregations, etc.) – Australia
    – Interviews. 3. Priests – Interviews. 4. Catholic
    Church – Australia – Clergy. 5. Monasticism and
    religious orders – Australia. I. Conference of
    Major Superiors (Australia). II. Title.
255'.0092'2

Acknowledgements

To be responsible for this project has been a pleasurable and rewarding experience, so I first acknowledge my gratitude to the National Major Superiors of religious men and women in Australia for entrusting it to me, especially to Brother Alman Dwyer, FMS, and his committee for their unfailing encouragement and belief in me. I thank Mark Cranfield, Officer in Charge, Oral History Department, Australian National Library, Canberra, for assistance and courteous patience far beyond the line of duty; Brian English, Lecturer, School of Social Work, University of New South Wales, Kensington, for generous help with statistical analysis; Monica Humphrey, Brisbane, for so willingly carrying the main burden of typing transcripts; the women, religious and lay, too numerous to name, who assisted with their typing expertise; and my friends for their interest in the project and their moral support.

Foreword

Publicly professing to having a distinctive lifestyle, known throughout the ages as 'religious life', is an extraordinarily challenging experience in the church today. Few would deny that this lifestyle is in a process of transformation.

Those involved in this transformative process have the opportunity of weighing up this experience, of reflecting on it, of dreaming new dreams and seeing new visions, of being involved in the evolution of a new future.

It is the particular responsibility of persons in leadership positions in any group that is involved in this transformation to nurture the members so they may have a vision for the moment, may perceive it in its history, in its complexity and in its possibility.

It was out of awareness of the responsibility that was theirs at this particular moment in the history of religious life in the church that the National Conference of the Major Superiors of the Religious of Australia at a National Assembly in May 1984 committed itself to a major project, a study of religious life in Australia.

The objectives of this project were historical, but more than historical. The focus of the study was to be the experience of those who were themselves living religious life at this particular period, rooted in a past that was loved, called into the challenges of a new present, and with the task of shaping a new future, while experiencing the self-questioning, the struggle and the uncertainty of such a transformative moment.

Religious life, however, is not simply a vocation for an individual. It is, and has always been, a gift for the whole community. Data having been gathered, it was therefore to be weighed and reflected upon by a variety of individuals and groups from the whole community, so that understandings might be deepened and new possibilities might be envisioned.

This project, carried through with great commitment by a National Committee of the Conference of Major Superiors and their researcher and project officer, Sister Naomi Turner,

CSB, is now at the moment of publication. The first volume, *Which Seeds Shall Grow?*, is a gathering together of the data, a telling of the experience of the subjects of this study: women and men religious. The second volume, *Men and Women in Religious Life*, is both commentary and reflection on this data from people who are involved in a broad spectrum of activity in our human community.

To all those women and men religious who have contributed, to the researcher, Sister Naomi, to the National Committee, to the commentators and those who have reflected on these questions, we express gratitude.

It would be their wish, and it is ours, as an Australian Conference of Major Superiors, that this study be of value in stimulating thought and discussion. May it play its part in the creation of a new future for religious life and for the church in Australia.

6 August 1988
Sister Helen Lombard
National President
Australian Conference of Major Superiors

Contents

This book is dedicated to the 100
religious women and 50 religious men
who shared with me some of their inmost
thoughts and the deepest experiences
of their lives.

Introduction 1

*A*t their annual conference in
1984 the National Major Superiors[1] of religious men and
women in Australia authorised a study on religious life in
Australia and nominated a committee to be responsible for
this. My work as project officer commenced late in 1985.

The objectives of this study include helping society as a
whole and the Catholic Church in particular—hierarchy,
clergy, laity—to understand the present meaning of religious
life as seen through the eyes of religious men and women
themselves; helping religious men and women reflect on their
own experiences as religious in order to reach a deeper
understanding of the meaning of their life; indicating the
shape and structure of religious life in the future.

The data for this study was obtained through interviews
with individual religious recorded on a reel-to-reel tape recorder.
The length of interviews, largely depending on the ease of
articulation of the interviewees, ranged from one of twenty
minutes to one of three and a half hours. The same basic
questions covered a variety of topics: early childhood background; reasons for entering a congregation[2]; novitiate training; vows of chastity, poverty and obedience; community
living; nature of ministry; the Catholic Church; aspects of
Australian society; values and attitudes of the individual
religious and the future of religious life.

The National Library of Australia supplied the recording
equipment, including the tapes used. From these tapes, typists
prepared the transcripts of interviews.

All religious congregations, male and female, were invited
to participate in the study. Four female congregations chose
not to accept the invitation: one of those four has just over

[Explanatory footnotes have been added for the benefit of
those unfamiliar with the terms used in religious life.]

1. A major superior is the person ultimately responsible for the overall
   administration of a religious province or of a total congregation of sisters,
   brothers or priests. The major superior is usually assisted by a council.
2. A congregation is the total group of religious—male or female—who have
   chosen to live by the constitutions, approved by the Holy See, of a specific
   founder or foundress. The constitutions are the rules by which the religious
   live.

three hundred members; the remaining three together have almost thirty. One brothers' congregation, with twenty-four members, did not participate; nor did three clerical congregations, one with just over one hundred members and the other two together comprising ten members. Each major superior nominated a contact person who supplied names of religious in respective congregations and gave relevant information concerning them.

Interviewees were chosen by a probability sampling in a two-stage process. Congregational lists of members were filed and members numbered consecutively, disregarding congregational divisions. Those members who were overseas were immediately excluded, but those on a year's leave of absence were included: this information was supplied by the contact person.

The total number of sisters, 10021, was arranged in thousands by random order and, using the random number tables, ten numbers were selected out of each thousand. The names of 100 sisters emerged. The same proportion, one in 100, was not used in the case of priests and brothers. The number of priests available was 1302, and that of brothers, including those belonging to clerical congregations[1], was 1838. For this particular study twenty-five from each group was considered the minimum number for viability. The random number tables were again used to select interviewees.

Among the group of sisters thus selected, four were unwilling to be interviewed, two were senile and so unable to participate, and four had left their congregations. Among the priests, only one was too ill to participate. Two brothers were unwilling to be interviewed and two others could not take part because of ill health. In each of the above cases the next religious on the list was chosen as replacement. Each interviewee was contacted by a letter in which the history and aims of the study were outlined, anonymity assured and an invitation to participate was given. Arrangements for the time and date of the interview were made; the place of the interview was normally the community house of the interviewee regardless of where it was in Australia.

1. The members of a clerical congregation are male, and are usually ordained as priests, but some members may choose to be non-ordained brothers.

Obtaining the data by semi-structured interviews offered me an opportunity to explore the complexities and richness in the lives of religious, but it limited my ability to isolate clear-cut, concise replies. I gained impressions from body language, facial expressions, tone of voice, silences and expressed emotions: these are clearly impossible to reduce to simple numbers or categories. However, these were by far the major factors that made the interviews revealing and memorable. Facts and generalisations presented in this study are, of course, related to what the 150 interviewees had to say, and so may in no way be interpreted as representative of all religious men and women in Australia. But, while not proving how all these religious men and women are thinking, they do point the direction of their thoughts.

Because of the above factors, which are inherent in the method chosen for this study, I cannot always indicate the precise support or otherwise given by religious to any one issue. Nor can I compile all the variety of replies to a question. So, where appropriate, I give more emphasis to those religious who indicate by their replies that they are moving from traditional patterns of thinking and living. This is not to denigrate in any degree the past. Religious life of thirty years ago can be too easily judged in the light of Vatican II documents: to do so would be very unjust. We are always people of our times, and we move forward only because of the strength of those behind us. Hence, if good and appropriate changes are now emerging in religious life, it is largely because of the valiant religious men and women who, within their period of history, grew in rich understanding of what it means to follow Christ. More importantly still, the older religious have provided the stable background and reference point against which it was possible to experiment with different forms of religious life after Vatican II. Since the customs and traditions of the past are well documented, I decided to give less emphasis to them in this particular study.

At this stage it is necessary to look more carefully not only at the changes within religious life, but also at the reasons behind these changes and, using their own words as much as possible, to try to discover why some religious today are very different from those of thirty years ago. The age of the individual religious has little to do with his/her views: one of the most far-sighted, clear thinking was a woman in her seventies, living within a traditional institution on a far-flung corner of the Australian coast.

A time for decision 2

I have interviewed 50 men and 100 women. The project for which I was employed necessitated my interviewing men and women who had professed their vows in various congregations in Australia. They are no longer names and numbers to me, but real people, many of whom with a clarity of soul and mind that is truly beautiful, and as such I wish to present them. Much has been written on the history of religious life, on the crossroads at which religious are said to stand today, on the possible future or demise of religious life and on the multitudinous reasons both for a definite future and for a definite demise. In this collation, however, my main aim is to show the humanity of these men and women, so many of whom trustingly told me about the warp and woof of their lives, revealing in simplicity their searchings, their dreams, their vulnerability. As much as possible, then, I shall use their own words to tell the stories where courage and beauty are poignantly visible through the handicaps, the misunderstandings and the joys that are part of the inevitable trappings of humanity.

Sisters

The women who entered the convent fall roughly into two divisions: those who from an early age knew that they would eventually become sisters, and those who, when they felt they had to enter, fought against it. The former always came from a fairly stable, loving family which had provided a religious atmosphere in the home. In one sister's family of eight children, for example, three became sisters and one a diocesan priest. As a child she had accompanied her mother on visits to four aunts in convents, where they had made much of her. She said: 'I always felt that the Lord was calling me to himself.' She entered happily at twenty-one with the full approval of her parents. Another, aged fifty-seven years, spoke of what is often called a good Catholic home:

> God was important in our family. My mother made a big effort now and again to get her seven children to say a family rosary, and we could never stay put longer than that. We said grace at

meals and my father, always before he went to bed, knelt into an armchair in the lounge room with his face to the back of the chair and said his night prayers.

An Irish sister in her mid-fifties came, as did many Irish sisters, from a home where the mother would speak about religious life and the wonderful opportunities it gave to serve God and to experience a peaceful life. But not all sisters came from comfortable or happy homes. A thirty-six-year-old sister remembered:

> . . . a hard background, because my mother became chronically ill, so that, from the age of ten, I had to cope with much of the housework and cooking. My father even looked to me to be an adult. I never really had a childhood from the age of ten onwards, but I was happy enough playing a role. It is only recently that I have learned that I didn't cope as well as I thought I did.

A forty-seven-year-old sister reflected:

> Overall, my childhood was stable, but there was a lot of unhappiness in it. My parents were totally incompatible and this resulted in great tension. I think that created a deep lack of confidence in myself, perhaps a great need for reassurance, perhaps a great fear of disapproval and distrust of people's affections.

And, coming from a broken home herself, a thirty-one-year-old sister commented:

> One of the old ideas was that people who entered religious life always came from a good family background and from a good, supporting kind of atmosphere. That's a misconception. Another is that people, when they enter religious life, are going to be totally integrated human beings. That is not the way life is. People are becoming less and less integrated and less and less whole, because society is so messed up. I can't see anywhere in the Gospels that the people whom Jesus invited fit that criteria. And, if the people who enter religious life don't have what has become the normal, everyday experiences of many, they are not going to be able to say anything to the world. They have to be people who have lived a variety of the ordinary everyday

9

experiences. When they come, yes, they are going to have wounds like everyone else, and we have to acknowledge that. And I think their real word to the world is that you can have those wounds and they can be healed, and that you can carry on. That is the biggest gift.

There are women who have come from other denominations to make their journey to religious life. One, born an Anglican, joined the Baptist then the Pentecostal churches before becoming a Catholic and entering a contemplative order[1] of sisters in her late twenties. An Anglican rectory was home for a sixty-year-old sister. About the age of seventeen, she became 'Intensely interested in different beliefs. I wasn't dissatisfied with the Anglican faith; it was really part of me, but I felt that there was something further that I had to look for.' When she became a Catholic at the age of twenty-one, her parents told her to leave home. It was a very difficult emotional time for her: 'It seemed to my Dad that I was throwing away what mattered most as far as he and my mother were concerned.' Soon afterwards she entered a convent, and it was some nine months later that he visited her as a novice.

He came to the convent and the novice mistress said to me: 'Your father is waiting to see you. He won't sit down or have a cup of tea—he demands to see you.' When I went in, he did not even look at me—he stood with his back to me and he said: 'If you forget all this nonsense and come home, we'll be just as we always were.' I waited until he had finished speaking, and I said to him: 'Listen, Dad, I've thought about this, and I've prayed about it for a long time, and I'm convinced I'm where God wants me to be. Do you want me to be anywhere else?'

And he turned around and he put out his hands and he called me by my name and said: 'If you are where God wants you to be, I wouldn't want you to be anywhere else.' Right from the time we were small children Dad would say to us: 'Pray to know the will of God, and then follow it no matter what it costs.' That had been

1. A contemplative order is one in which the members take solemn vows, and exercise their ministry of prayer and work within the enclosure of their property's walls. The members of an active religious congregation take simple vows (which are less binding) and usually work with the laity in hospitals, schools, etc.

bred into us right throughout the years, and I suppose that was why he reacted as he did then. He never said another word against my vocation after that.

Some sisters had childhood experiences that greatly influenced them as mature adults. An Italian sister remembered her father sending the family to the south of Italy for safety during World War II.

There, unfortunately, the situation was worse, because the Germans were retreating and they bombed all the houses in our village. We had to walk to the next village through heavy snow. My mother carried the baby, while my brother and I walked beside her. My brother, who was two years of age, died from the intense cold of that journey.

A seventy-four-year-old sister looked back to World War I:

My father was working in Romania in 1916 when all English-speaking people were told to evacuate. It was a matter of leaving literally everything. My mother carried a pillow slip with a few things in it, and we went by cattle truck to Russia. I was four and an only child. I was terribly upset, because I wasn't able to take my kitten with me. The whole episode had a profound effect on me: since then I have never been bothered if I was moved from one place to another. In a way, I feel I am always on the move.

More than one Irish girl came to Australia to join a congregation before her seventeenth birthday. Irish sisters home in Ireland from working in Australia would visit schools to speak to the girls about the mission in Australia. 'They were canvassing recruits', was the comment by one Irish sister who remembered as a young girl showing interest in the sisters. They spoke privately to her on several occasions before giving her a letter to take home to her parents requesting an interview with them. This was the first the parents knew of her wish to enter a convent. Within a fortnight of the interview between parents and sisters, the girl was on a boat to Australia, there to enter a juniorate, which was a boarding school exclusively for those intending to enter religious life at the end of their schooling. She was fourteen years of age.

11

I believed I was coming out to serve God. It was twenty years before I realised I was really running away from home, where, since my mother was more or less an invalid, I had to take a lot of responsibility for a family of eight children. It took me a long time to come to terms with that.

Usually, as was the case for a fifty-six-year-old sister, Irish parents considered a vocation in their family a great honour. But a seventy-six-year-old sister recalled the sadness of her father:

He did not want me to enter and leave Ireland, especially as I was just seventeen, but no Irish parent in those days could say 'No' to a child wanting to become a religious. They felt God was calling, and it was their duty to support the vocation.

A sister in her late forties had wanted to enter at the age of sixteen. Her parents forbade her to do so until the mother remembered that a young girl of seventeen had died within a month of her parents' refusal to permit her to enter a convent. 'If we don't let her go,' she told her husband, 'God will take her from us.'

Few parents in Australia were entirely happy with their daughters' decision to become a religious. A ninety-year-old sister became a little emotional when she spoke about her father:

Throughout my sixteenth year I was fighting against the feeling I should enter. When a sister asked me if I would enter, I told her I didn't have a dowry, because I thought that would be a good way to get out of it. But she said: 'You have the dowry God gave you. You have health, strength, intelligence. That's all you need.' At this time, there were three girls in the home and my father had us take it in turn to play the piano and sing for him when he came home for midday lunch. This particular day it was my turn and I was playing and singing. He came over and put his hand on my shoulder and said: 'You would never leave me to go to a convent, would you?' I said: 'Yes, that is what I'd like to do.' He was very distressed and upset. My mother, however, was on my side, and I entered at sixteen. I used to write to my father almost every fortnight, and my mother later told me that he kept all my letters unopened in his office. He did not come to see me until my first profession, three years later. After that you couldn't keep him away.

Another sister of forty entered at the age of twenty-one against her mother's wishes. It was fourteen years before they were reconciled. A sixty-two-year-old sister came into contact with sisters for the first time when, at sixteen, she applied for work in a convent. During the interview the superior asked if she would like to enter religious life and do domestic work. 'Being young and shy and thinking my mother would be pleased, I said I would.' The next day she was received as a postulant. It was to take some forty years before she made a free, informed decision to stay.

Many people will consider it strange that a girl, feeling she would prefer not to do so, voluntarily enters a convent. Yet more than half the sisters interviewed spoke about fighting to escape from what they call a vocation. A forty-seven-year-old sister was fifteen when the religious principal of her school asked if she had ever thought of being a sister. Very quickly she told her she would never dream of it:

> But the awful part was that the thought wouldn't go away after that. To me it was awful because I didn't want to leave home and the exciting life that seemed to be opening up to me. I didn't want to be confined in a convent. I didn't talk about it to anyone for a couple of years, because I thought it might go away, like a headache. Then, after a year at university, I entered. By that time I felt very strongly it was what God wanted, and a part of me wanted it, too.

This strong feeling that God was calling them into religious life is common to the majority of sisters. It was a feeling they found difficult to describe. Many resonated with a forty-seven-year-old sister who said:

> I entered at nineteen, because there was something in me that wouldn't let me forget about the idea. I half hoped that I would find out that I wasn't suited to the life, but I wasn't free to ignore the idea: there was something right in the depths of my being that said I had to give this a go.

A thirty-nine-year-old sister confessed:

> A lot of things about religious life didn't appeal to me: the buildings, the clothes the sisters wore, the restrictions on their life in terms of relationships with family and friends. But, when it came to the point, those things were not significant. There was something that went beyond them. I know I wanted to help the poor. I know I had a pervasive sense of God, and I had always wanted to be very good. I think I came to see religious life as being *the* way of making a complete commitment to God. For me today, religious life embodies a special call to a special relationship with God.

After graduating from university at the age of twenty-three, a sister now in her sixties, recalled:

> I felt a very distinct call to the congregation I finally joined. It came from the depth of my own being. At the same time, I felt a distinct and very strong revulsion. I didn't have a desire to enter, but I did have a sense of rightness about it. I am still convinced it was the right step for me.

A thirty-six-year-old sister who had entered at eighteen said that a number of forces had brought her to religious life.

> It was a combination of an idealistic personality, the whole cultural environment of commitment and causes of the sixties, as well as being in a situation where I saw all that being embodied in my religious teachers. My main motive was to do something for God.

One motive for joining a religious congregation was a realisation that what the world was offering was not really what she wanted. At seventeen, a fifty-nine-year-old sister had been invited to her first party with soldiers.

> I was so excited and looked forward to it. We had a wonderful night, and then I remember going home on the Manly ferry, looking at the water and thinking: 'There must be something more than this. I've experienced the most exciting thing in my life and yet it still doesn't satisfy me.'

Four sisters were engaged to be married before they decided to enter religious life. They said that they finally realised that marriage was not for them. A number of factors influenced a twenty-nine-year-old to enter five years ago: she is still working through her reasons for choosing to become a sister.

When I was a child, I was sexually abused over a long period by a member of the family. The first time I spoke about it was to a young man who wanted to marry me. I finally told him why I couldn't successfully handle the physical side of our relationship. I faced a whole lot of questions then. Was I normal? A year later I thought seriously about entering a convent. I was very insecure and trying to find out the reasons for things. I was a nurse, and I remember an unconscious eighteen-year-old girl was brought into casualty. I was with her for the four hours the doctor was working on her. She never recovered. I saw a lot of myself in that girl: I was looking at my own fragility, and I didn't have any answers. Basically, I would have to say my motives for entering were essentially a concern for people. I wanted to have more time for people.

The great majority of sisters joined the congregation responsible for their education, many joining immediately their schooling ended. Some looked elsewhere for different reasons. A sister in her mid-fifties was attracted to the one she joined because it was so large she thought she would be able to leave it easily if she found she had made the wrong decision. Another in her early forties found a brochure with addresses of many congregations. She wrote to each one.

Then it was a process of elimination. I got rid of those replies in which my name was spelled incorrectly and those letters that were too stiff and starchy. I turned to the congregation I finally joined because, although I had addressed the letter to them in Sydney, their reply was written on a page with a country letterhead and it was posted in Melbourne. I thought I would fit in with those sisters because they seemed odd enough: they weren't perfect and neither was I.

Brothers

Where religious women volunteered considerable detail about their background, their feelings about a vocation and their parents' reactions, men, especially the brothers, were usually nonchalantly brief. Except for two migrants, one arriving in Australia at the age of three, the other at nine, all brothers interviewed were born in Australia. All were born into Catholic families except one who at five years was baptised a Catholic when his mother remarried. Two brothers reported unhappy childhoods; one, illegitimate, was reared by his aunt, while the mother of the second was a migrant widow who had married a man emotionally affected by the war and unable to communicate with his stepson, whose values, as an Australian, were vastly different from those of his parents.

A brother now in his seventies was thirteen when a sister in charge of his class asked who was interested in becoming a brother. He had never seen a brother, but, for a reason he cannot remember, he indicated his interest. His mother understandably was not very pleased, but his father and Irish grandparents happily transferred him to a juniorate. Another brother in his seventies was fifteen when he transferred from school to juniorate. He, too, was uncertain about his reasons:

> I had been at boarding school for four years and, of course, I admired the men who were working in a tough environment in those days. Another factor was that because of the depression there was no future for me on my father's farm. Both my parents were happy at my decision.

A brother in his thirties joined a juniorate at the age of sixteen, because he wanted to help others through teaching. He recollected: 'I later heard that, when my mother saw my bed in the juniorate, she went home and cried and cried—it was so narrow.' A brother in his forties entered the juniorate at sixteen.

> One reason for wanting to be a brother was the desire to save my soul, another was my admiration for the prayerfulness of the brothers. And, at that stage, I was frightened of my own sexuality.

I remember reading that one had a better chance of saving one's soul as a religious. I have been unlearning that dictum ever since.

His parents were pleased with his decision, especially as his school did not include the two senior classes: 'A lot of boys', he said, 'went on to the juniorate to complete their education.' The juniorate was for all a happy place, very like a boarding school, except there were more prayers and the boys were allowed home for only six weeks during the Christmas holidays.

The major reason for young men entering the religious life was a deep admiration for their teachers coupled with a desire to teach: 68 per cent of brothers joined the congregation of brothers who had taught them. A brother in his fifties spoke for several when he said: 'The men in the congregation were happy teaching, and that's what I wanted to do. I also had the idea of doing something for Christ.' Of the brothers, 24 per cent did not enter from school. One had become interested in religious life at the age of twenty-five, after seeing a Catholic life exhibition in Melbourne where different congregations displayed material. He thought: 'I'll give it a go—I've nothing to lose.' A brother in his fifties had left school at thirteen. When he was sixteen, a workmate who often accompanied him to church asked why he did not become a lay brother. He said:

I had previously thought of religious life, but I believed my lack of education would have prevented it, as I had never heard of lay brothers. The moment this chap asked me, a special feeling came within me that has lasted to the present day. So I joined the brothers exactly three weeks later.

The remaining brothers entered the novitiate within one or two years of leaving school.

Priests

Four priests were already ordained when they came to Australia. At thirteen a Filipino priest joined the juniorate of his congregation. His reasons had nothing to do with the spiritual: 'I wanted to get away from the confines of my family, to join the group of nineteen boys leaving from my school and to see a new place.'

The third in a family of seven, one Irish priest was eleven when his mother died, leaving his father to rear the family. Before he had finished his secondary schooling, he was apprenticed to a furrier. At the age of twenty-three he made a retreat given in a monastery of the congregation he was to enter. The idea of being a priest had been vaguely with him since childhood, and, 'impressed by these very holy men dressed in their religious habits and by their very beautiful singing of the Divine Office', he asked to join them. Because of his lack of education they accepted him as a religious brother. Four years later he asked and was refused permission to study for the priesthood. After eleven years he was sent to the missions as catechist and part-time administrator. Seven years later—after another and successful request—he began studies for the priesthood at the age of forty-five.

When he was sixteen, the second Irish priest applied to two religious congregations, but was not accepted. After finishing his secondary education he became a labourer until he joined the army at twenty and went through military college. Because his family needed his financial support, he did not enter until he was twenty-seven. His reasons were vague: 'At that time you didn't go in so much for specific reasons; it was more following an instinct.'

A Dutch priest in his late fifties was influenced by his war experiences. Refusing to co-operate with the German army, his father was imprisoned for a time and then could obtain only a poorly paid job. When the priest was thirteen, he fell from his bicycle in front of a speeding German truck. Swerving to avoid him, the German driver crashed into a shop.

Dad sent me with a box of the best cigars to the corporal. I didn't want to go, but Dad said he had risked his own life to save mine. He later came to our home and Mum cooked a meal for him. The incident helped to balance my views, so I didn't see all Germans as hostile.

To avoid being recruited by the Germans at seventeen he, with other boys, crossed to the allied armies, where he served in the Red Cross as stretcher boy and interpreter. He said:

> As Red Cross men, we weren't supposed to take any prisoners, but I often picked up wounded Germans and took them to our hospital. I also led back about twenty Germans sick and tired of the war.

At the end of the war he joined his congregation: 'I don't know exactly why I did, but I'd had the idea of being a priest since I was about fourteen.'

A priest in his sixties recalled a lesson his father had taught him:

> Because I went to a school outside our diocese in the depression years when Catholic schools were struggling to survive, the bishop removed my father from all his parish positions. My father continued to be a daily communicant, saying, 'Bishops can sometimes make mistakes.' After Vatican II, when tensions and pressure surrounded decisions that had to be made, I looked back to my father's experience, and it was a great help to me.

Only two men experienced family protests and attempts to change their minds when they opted for the priesthood. Said one: 'They trundled girls in and out of the house for a year. I just let it ride. There was no use arguing.' Some had thought of joining the diocesan clergy, but, realising their family could not finance them, they turned to religious congregations. A priest in his seventies recalled the situation at the time he entered: 'Bishops were then saying from the pulpits that they weren't taking any more vocations as they couldn't finance them. A priest told me to try a religious congregation.'

The majority of priests had thought of ordination from an early age: 'Priests in our parish', said one in his fifties, 'often used to talk to the boys about becoming priests, so we were always conscious of this option.' By the time they entered religious life, their reasons were varied. One in his sixties who had served in the war explained:

The general uncertainty of the times influenced me. I read the Catholic Truth Society pamphlets, and they spelt out the advantages of the religious life. The security appealed to me. The war had taught me that life had nothing of a permanent nature to offer. It was as simple as that.

Others too looked for something substantial. A priest in his thirties said: 'Religious life seemed to be both philosophically and religiously good, and I wanted to get closer to God. At that stage, to be a priest seemed the best way.' Another priest in his thirties had worked for three years in a bank.

I decided to enter from complete and utter dissatisfaction with the kind of life I was leading. Self-centred and intent on getting more money, I was really dissatisfied and unhappy underneath, so I decided to give the religious life a go.

One man came from the far outback of Queensland to join a contemplative congregation. His studies in history and literature at university had helped him to think more seriously about human life. Philosophy encouraged him to ask questions: 'What was I going to do with my life that would make sense at the end of it?' Originally intending to be a missionary, he read an autobiography of a contemplative brother, felt in empathy with him and joined his congregation. A diocesan priest influenced another man when he was in his early teens:

He was an Irishman, friendly with our family and he often shared a meal with us. But his prayerfulness impressed me the most. I'd drop into the church about 5 p.m. and Father Joe was always there, praying in the front pew.

The reasons for entering were not always fulfilled. One priest joined a missionary congregation because, after reading *Far East* magazines as a boy and listening to teachers telling him that the future lay with Asia, he hankered to go to China. Forty-eight years later he set foot in China as a temporary visitor. One priest in his mid-thirties is struggling to ascertain whether he had made a fully free commitment to religious life:

I have a certain bitterness towards my parents and the Catholic Church. Because I was part of that family and Church, my vision of the world outside that small community was limited. I now look back and wish I had known about the number of options that were available to me at the time I entered. At fifteen my parents were debating whether I should finish secondary schooling, and I said I was thinking of becoming a priest. That decided them, so there was then a certain expectation on me. The priests at the school encouraged vocations, so things just seemed to happen without much thought on my part.

Conclusion

The men, especially the brothers, largely saw their vocation in terms of ministry: women rarely mentioned the influence of a particular ministry on their decision to enter a convent. Not one person interviewed referred to wealth in family background: one brother spoke about his well-to-do family.

Not for brothers and priests the questioning of girls doubting a religious vocation. The motives of brothers were clear-cut and practical: they wanted to teach; they admired the brothers who taught them; they liked the lifestyle they saw and it was—occasionally it appeared as a bonus—something for Christ, or they could save their souls more easily. The motives of priests varied a little more: some were influenced at an early age; others at a later age saw the life as a worthwhile service. Not one brother or priest mentioned, as so many sisters did, that he had ever felt either an instinctive dislike of entering religious life or a strong inner compulsion to do so.

Novitiate 3

Sisters

*W*hile sisters were speaking about their childhood and family, they often became thoughtfully, happily pensive. They smiled at memories recalled. When the topic of their novitiate was being discussed, stronger and negative emotions visibly surfaced. Only two sisters acknowledged that the three-year period as postulant[1] and novice[2] was a very happy one for them: one was three years professed[3], and her novitiate was totally at variance with that of almost all the sisters; the other was in her late eighties and I wondered whether it was for her a case of rose-coloured glasses. The contemplative sisters told me that their novitiate differed from community life in one respect: as novices they had more contact with their superior, the novice mistress. All sisters interviewed, except three, had taken their final vows: these three spoke about their spiritual formation where the others spoke about their novitiate training.

The two terms, spiritual formation and novitiate training, reveal two differing worlds of values. Within their own families and at school the majority of young women entering religious life learnt to have a respect for themselves and their individuality, to be self-confident, to relate socially with those they met, and to assume responsibilities appropriate to their age. For those entering religious life in recent years this personal development, especially in their relationship with God, was encouraged to deepen and broaden into full maturity. Those in charge of their formation hoped they would come to their ministry as fully prepared adults, able to work with the freedom of professionals, yet in consultation with the leaders of their congregation. But those who entered in earlier years were trained by practices to learn new attitudes and new patterns of living: the novitiate for them was an upside-down

---

1. A person taking a live-in look at a religious community before officially seeking membership on a trial basis.
2. One who has commenced training in a religious order or congregation.
3. Profession is the religious ceremony at which one takes temporary vows of chastity, poverty and obedience. Final profession is when these vows are taken for life.

24

world of values. Within three years most had learned to accept these values, at least externally, while a few absorbed them so completely that today they still believe in them. Their training had as an objective their socialisation into a religious congregation organised to service an institution, school or hospital. This socialisation meant that the needs of the religious were subordinated to the needs of the institution. Hierarchical leadership and a common life in which all shared the same ministerial activity, timetable, clothes, food and recreation ensured that the institution had a supply of obedient, undemanding and mobile personnel. Because ninety-three sisters in this study (excluding the four contemplative sisters interviewed) experienced the latter, at least in some degree, this report concentrates on the novitiate training, which scarcely altered in its basic principles up to 1970. Even in the first half of the 1970s little fundamental change was visible in the majority of congregations.

Some sisters did not want to talk at length about their novitiate experience: it was too painful for them. Others were often close to tears or in tears as they recalled their first years in the convent. A few were frankly angry about their experiences and with those who had been in authority over them. It was very evidently a time that had affected them deeply, and, as I listened to their stories, I became saddened that young women had undergone such trials; and, as the interview continued, I marvelled that so many had triumphed over their beginnings in religious life. What helped them to do so was their acceptance that their novitiate training was simply part of the religious culture of their time, a culture in which those in authority over them also had been caught.

On their arrival at the convent the young women changed into postulant's clothes. A forty-year-old sister recalled:

It was a boiling hot day, and here we were dressing up in dreadful, thick, black dresses. The novice mistress said our dresses were too short. I looked at mine and it was well below the knees, but I had a bit of a hem and I thought I could let that down. But the next day a piece was actually added to the bottom of the dress.

A thirty-five-year-old sister's immediate reaction to life in the novitiate was that it was 'quite quaint for the first two weeks and after that I couldn't believe it was real'. A forty-one-year-old sister felt she was in a prison:

> I could not believe the things that were happening. It was like a Shakespearean performance. At dinner, for instance, we each had a tin bowl and ate our soup, main meal and our dessert from it. I thought: 'My God, wait until I tell my friends.'

A sixty-four-year-old sister had seen herself walking into another period of history: 'One of the most difficult things for me was the question of hygiene. We could have one bath a week, and that was taken through the day in an allotted ten minutes.' Another sister in her seventies had had the luxury of two baths a week: 'At night we would put hot water into our dishes in the dormitory, but the water would be cold by the time we went to bed forty-five minutes later.' Another sister said that they were allowed to change their clothes only twice a week: unofficially she often changed them more frequently.

The days were strictly regimented. Some rose at 5.30 a.m., others a little later. A fifty-five-year-old sister remembers her first morning as Dickensian: 'I woke to the sound of a loud cow bell. It was like the crack of doom. I staggered to the window to see fog and mist. There was a graveyard outside, and I thought: "O my God, what have I done?"'

Mass and long prayers in common were before breakfast. Study, housework and prayers, each beginning and ending at regulated times, filled the day itself. As a fifty-five-year-old commented: 'We couldn't even decide when to go to bed.' One sister in her fifties who entered expecting and not finding bare boards for beds found great difficulty in asking permissions for little essential things such as using a new cake of soap.

Physical work was taxing, especially for sisters completely engaged in domestic work. 'I found it slog, slog all the time,' reflected a fifty-three-year-old sister. 'I don't know what the hell I stayed for, and I wouldn't go through it again. But I still feel I am in the right place.' Another sister in her sixties was frequently so weary that she would pray earnestly to get a cold in order to have a little more time in bed in the mornings.

Structures were all-important. A forty-six-year-old was sceptical about the value of them:

> The novices who were up earliest and had their stations of the cross said before morning prayers were held up as models. I always had my suspicions about that. I did it once or twice but it had no meaning for me. What I found most difficult was the mass conformity, that tremendously high regard for the voice of God calling us through every bell, no matter what. Holiness in religious life boiled down to how well you could adjust yourself to be on time all the time.

Those who had entered straight from school accepted the structures most readily. As a young postulant, a seventy-one-year-old sister told her novice mistress that she had understood the novitiate would be very difficult, but she was finding it easy. 'I made that huge mistake in my third week. It meant that for the next twelve months I certainly learnt all about hardships.'

For a contemplative sister, structures of the timetable meant conscientious adherence to those in European convents: 'We really kept the letter of the law. We rose an hour later in the summer and an hour earlier in the winter. It was too bad Australian seasons were the opposite of those in Europe.'

All postulants and novices were anxious to do the right thing, and their anxiety ensured the training would be effective. A forty-nine-year-old sister 'conformed like crazy because I would be sent home if I didn't'. A forty-four-year-old sister had fear as a constant companion: 'Fear was always with me in the novitiate. It was the fear of doing the wrong thing, of being corrected.' A seventy-eight-year-old sister remembered the tension she used to feel:

> I felt a constant tension because everything had to be done in a certain way and in a great hurry: everything was so important and I couldn't reconcile myself with the tension accompanying ordinary things such as preparing a breakfast for someone.

27

As a forty-two-year-old sister said simply: 'I was glad when I was in bed and safe from being hounded.' A forty-six-year-old sister commented:

> If you didn't conform you felt guilty; yet sometimes when you did conform you felt uneasy because it was something you believed was not quite right — for example, not speaking in silence time to a sister who was crying.

Lack of privacy hurt most sisters: they especially did not like their letters to and from their families being read. One seventy-six-year-old sister said: 'I was naturally shy, and the most difficult thing for me was to realise everyone in the novitiate knew almost everything about me.' Others became upset about the trauma resulting from an accidently broken cup as, according to a fifty-nine-year-old sister, 'it was so out of proportion with the incident and so out of character with any sort of love of God'.

Older sisters disliked the chapter of faults over which the novice mistress presided and publicly corrected the novices. A thirty-year-old sister found this chapter of faults replaced in her novitiate with a weekly group meeting during which the novices could mention grievances they had experienced during the past week. It was something she saw as un-Christian.

> Sometimes I would not have realised I had hurt someone until she brought it up publicly in the group. That a person would worry about something for four or five days, then talk about it in public, was hard for me to understand. It was like a violence and an invasion of privacy. My father had always said never to let the sun go down on your anger, so I could not understand why sisters would simmer over something for so long.

For some, the culture shock on entering the novitiate was very disturbing. One sister in her forties was unhappy being anonymous in a crowd. 'I felt my individuality had disappeared. For one thing my red hair was no longer visible as I wore a veil. I was average size and a quieter person than most, so blended too easily with the group.' Another sister in her forties said:

As far as I could see they were trying to destroy an individuality in us, to make us conform to some idea of a good sister. The things that made women most beautiful and the gifts they had had to be destroyed. They made life hard for them. They tried to break them. They didn't trust them. It was a terrible shock to find that we were not encouraged to make friends.

A sister in her mid-thirties also found rules discouraging friendships:

We had strict rules about relationships. No opportunity for communication between two or three sisters was given. When two sisters became friendly, they would be forbidden to speak to one another. That was devastating for young women, when they had no idea of the fear of lesbianism that lay behind the command.

A fifty-year-old sister agreed: 'We were very muddled about what was called "particular friendships". We couldn't understand why we couldn't be friends.' Even recreation was designed to prevent friendships developing. Within some congregations the sisters, unable to choose their companions, always sat in order of seniority; within others, the sisters recreated in small circular groups that were constantly changed. Human ingenuity occasionally found a way to thwart the system. A sixty-five-year-old sister reported: 'If two sisters really wanted to talk together, each would sit at the same edge of two circles and converse back to back.' Sisters sometimes made an opportunity to speak to one another in silence time, but the guilt this occasioned in them and the fear of being caught made such occasions rare.

A sub-culture was deliberately fostered. The novitiate was a time for learning to be a sister, especially in outward behaviour. Natural courtesies — such as greeting a sister with 'Good morning' — lapsed because of the silence expected, and as a forty-one-year-old sister noted: 'The law became more important than a person.' Novices would show the new postulant how things were done, how they were expected to respond. A sister in her fifties had always felt under the eyes of sisters: 'Even the way you stood while you were having morning tea was noted.' The sub-culture contained Victorian features. When a sister, now seventy-three, was told on her second day as a postulant to take a bath wearing a chemise, she questioned her novice mistress: 'How the heck can you clean yourself properly?' She quickly learnt that was not the way a postulant spoke to her novice mistress. Customs could seem strange at first, but postulants, with the example of novices before them, soon came to accept them. As a sixty-three-year-old sister explained: 'Among ourselves we laughed about such ridiculous things as kissing the floor when you were corrected. It took some of the sting out of the humiliation.'

One sister who entered as a twenty-seven-year-old felt like a child trying to start life again:

> I had to learn to be silent, not to talk about worldly things, not to be attached to one person, not to be vain. I remember placing soap between my clothes in the press so they would smell nice. One day I came to my cubicle to find my clothes strewn over my bed. Later the novice mistress lectured me on the vanity of putting soap among my clothes.

A sister who entered religious life in 1974 had been responsible in her job for an annual budget of $75,000. She said: 'Suddenly I couldn't make a decision about how to bleach serviettes. I found that absolutely devastating, and it wasn't the done thing to protest.' Initiative was squashed. Young women lost their self-confidence. A forty-eight-year-old sister recalled her experience.

> When I left the novitiate I felt I could do nothing. Before I entered I played the piano in public concerts. After the novitiate it worried me to play the organ for hymns. I was so fearful of making mistakes.

More than one echoed a fifty-seven-year-old sister: 'Even today I demand an impossible perfection of myself and others in little things.' A seventy-two-year-old sister summarised what many reported:

> We regressed as women. We were treated as children and expected to do as we were told and not to think for ourselves. The

world shrank to the boundaries of the convent and school, and we really didn't give thought to people outside.

As another sister remarked: 'We had to get permission to move from one room to another.' It was no wonder that sisters saw themselves acting as robots or cogs in a machine.

Sisters entering the convent before 1975 (approximately) can identify with much of what has been written about the novitiate. However, those who entered from the late 1960s found some relaxation within traditional training; but they also found their novitiate very difficult for two reasons. One: they were now better educated and so more actively questioning, less inclined to passive acceptance of God's will as revealed to them by their novice mistress. Two: religious life was no longer stable; change and uncertainty were in the air.

A sister entering in the late 1960s experienced 'incredible disillusionment'. She had been very involved in the Young Catholic Students' Movement on a national level, had studied and discussed all the Vatican II documents. Then, as a novice, she found she had to spend hours copying, word for word, outdated books on the scriptures. She became frustrated and angry at what seemed to her 'very childish, very ignorant ways of forming me as a religious'. Another sister who entered in 1970 said:

> We had nothing to hang on to because all was in flux. There were no set constitutions.[1] We didn't know what the future would be like, and neither did the novice mistress. It was unsettling. It was like signing a blank cheque at profession. We always seemed to be waiting for a definite ruling on something or another.

By the 1980s most congregations had adopted formation principles that radically altered the novitiate. A young woman entering religious life six years ago thoroughly enjoyed her time in formation.

---

1. Constitutions, as previously mentioned, are the rules (approved by Rome) by which a particular order or congregation of religious sisters lives.

From the time I entered, I had a real sense of belonging to my congregation and I was excited and hopeful for the future. I lived with another postulant and a novice in a house with older sisters in the community, and to me that was good and balanced. Community doesn't only consist of young people. When we were asked where we'd like to go for work experience, I asked to go to a very structured community, because I wanted to know something of the past, what the sisters had struggled through.

During my canonical year I was able to draw up my own programme, which the novice mistress approved. At the end of canonical year we celebrated by attending the opening of the Entertainment Centre in Sydney. We had to chuckle about that, wondering if there were other novices in the stalls. My novice mistress was my friend. She supported me in whatever happened. In whatever I did she stood by me, and she allowed me to make mistakes. I was treated as a responsible, mature woman, and I felt liberated. We saw our relatives as freely as we wanted to. My sister often came down to Sydney, parked her car in our backyard, came in and had lunch with us before going into town to shop. It was like a normal house.

When a sister of twenty-five entered, she had a few adjustments to make.

I felt pretty special. They hadn't had anyone for a few years, and here I was, I'd entered. The community paid me special attention for a while, then I became one of the mob. Initially that came as a shock. I missed very much the intimacy of my family, an intimacy not possible in religious life. I had to change some of my social habits and to fit in with something already there.

Another sister who entered in the last seven years had a rational approach to the difficulties she found in the novitiate.

The problem for me was finding people in the novitiate who had a set view of religious life. I couldn't see how you could make definite rules in a changing world. It never worried me that they had structures, only that they were not willing to see if they needed changing. You can't have a structure as an end in itself. I agreed to wear a veil from practicality. I said to myself: 'Why are we talking about this? It is a waste of energy. They will have to change one day.'

32

Where older sisters who had entered before the 1980s had emphasised the physical hardships, the humiliations and the traditions which, as they said, robbed them of maturity, the three young women who had entered in or after 1980 mentioned none of these. They had been recognised as mature women who needed certain guidance, but who were capable of making their own decisions, so assuming responsibility for themselves. They were active in their own spiritual formation.

Why did not the young women living in tension and fear in pre-1980 novitiates return to their homes? Often warned by the professed sisters they knew and liked, they came to the novitiate prepared for difficulties and determined to endure them for the three years of what they saw as their testing time. Other factors existed. The majority respected, admired and often liked their novice mistresses, women caught between normal human reactions and the demands placed upon them in their role. Even when novices were being corrected, many instinctively felt they were cared for and liked. As a seventy-year-old sister said:

> Although our novice mistress was a little harsh with us, we knew she was in a role. I could see beneath the role and could be myself with her. She didn't have great expectations of me that I couldn't meet. She allowed each of us to be ourselves. She was a very human woman and deeply spiritual.

When she was in the novitiate in the 1970s, a sister found her novice mistress unsympathetic and severe. In her second year this sister was replaced by another:

> She gave us an overwhelming sense that she loved us. That was our crying need — to know we were still individual human beings. I had lost all sense of who I was and she restored that to me. She challenged me to be myself.

Concerts were regular features in novitiate life, and more than once novices did a skit on happenings within the novitiate, including the doings and sayings of the novice mistress. As one sister said: 'She took it in good part and laughed. I suppose we were able to accept a lot of things because we knew novice mistresses were human and enjoyed a good joke.'

Personality differences meant that some did not feel a kinship with their novice mistress, but they knew professed sisters who became models for them and a sign of hope that things would be better once they were professed. One sister remarked: 'The sisters I loved and appreciated were real, individual people, full of fun. So I believed that once I had endured the novitiate, I would be myself again.' This was another factor. Although novices accepted and went along with the customs of the novitiate, they did not always believe in their value or see them as essential to religious life. For novices in the 1970s they had only to be accepted for the time of the novitiate. When a sister now in her thirties was finding life difficult as a novice, young professed sisters would whisper to her: 'It won't be long before your profession. Hang in there. Things will change.'

A few found their own ways to release the tension within them. A thirty-seven-year-old sister acted exactly as she was expected to do but, occasionally, 'I liked to have fun and I would get into mischief. For example, I would pinch the cigarettes out of the priest's cupboard and a couple of us would go down the back and smoke them.'

A sixty-four-year-old sister stayed in religious life because 'There was a core in the life that was true and right for me—all my difficulties were unfortunate necessities. The religious life was very much a relational thing between God and me.' A forty-seven-year-old sister always sensed she was in the right place: 'I loved the parts where my spirit was free and that was the spiritual part.'

The prayer life was appreciated by all sisters. As a forty-one-year-old sister explained: 'It was a very beautiful part of my life and that side of me developed.' A sister in her early fifties reflected:

Looking back I can see lasting values instilled into us. We must have consciously or unconsciously recognised that. There was the value of the primacy of a relationship with God and prayer as a means to that. There was a sense of service, especially to the underprivileged, given to us. Those values were important. All the other things were merely trappings of an age.

This deep appreciation for prayer and the opportunities for it the novitiate provided are two of the major reasons for novices remaining in otherwise harsh circumstances.

Another important factor was, as a sister in her forties explained: 'The good feeling of being with people who were like-minded. For the first time I was with people who all shared the same ideals and wanted to give themselves to Christ.' One after the other, sisters spoke warmly of their companions in the novitiate, and this despite the external restrictions placed on friendship by those in authority. The friendship of the novices, to use one sister's words, 'was a means of survival for me'. And difficult as it may be to believe considering the conditions within the novitiate, many sisters told me that, in the depths of their being, they were, as one said, 'at home'.

When sisters were asked directly why they had stayed in the novitiate, the usual reply was that they did not know, but, in common with a forty-four-year-old sister, most spoke about a compelling force urging them to continue. 'Something more than myself kept me there,' said a sister in her sixties.

Looking back, [added another in her sixties] you wonder how any reasonable and intelligent women could have lived through our experiences. We probably were so enculturated that we were unaware of the rather outlandish types of things we were doing. The old type of penances still existed that were not only meaningless but demeaning. I suppose we were not quite brainwashed, but influenced by the way the congregation thought of those things.

A sister thirty years younger had deliberately established a support system among her novice companions. They were caught in the traditional customs of a novitiate and, as well, realised that those in charge of their formation were incompetent: 'It was almost as if we decided consciously that we as persons and our values would not be destroyed.' When asked what made her remain, she replied:

It is a great mystery to me. I have absolutely no memory of making a rational decision about it. Absolutely none at all. I think I so badly wanted to be a religious that it was almost like a blind instinctual decision to stay.

Brothers

The novitiate period for the majority of sisters usually consisted of six to nine months as a postulant and two years as a novice. Most brothers, on the other hand, were postulants for something like nine weeks and novices for one year, and then were transferred to the scholasticate for a period of training in their profession as teachers. Since the average sister spent at least two and a half years in the novitiate, while the brother was there for half that period, coupled with the fact that 72 per cent of brothers were in novitiates situated in beautiful country areas, frequently on a farm, help to explain why brothers' reaction to novitiate life are very different from those of sisters.

Other factors contributed to the different reaction: 76 per cent of brothers, moving directly from juniorate or school to the novitiate, were continuing much the same lifestyle they had always led; their physical surroundings gave them great freedom of movement and, judging from the brothers' emphasis, the real saving grace was the time allotted to sport—this varied from three to six afternoons a week. Recreations for sisters consisted of walking in convent grounds or sitting in well-defined rows of seniority with hands occupied in some kind of sewing.

It is not surprising, therefore, that only three brothers experienced great difficulty during their novitiate. A brother in his fifties found it too regimented with little free time and no choice offered in sports. Another brother in his late fifties who had entered at nineteen did not like the silence and missed reading newspapers and listening to the radio. He was the only one to admit that he could not go through the novitiate again. Yet he did not appear to remember great traumas. He said: 'It was a challenging time and I enjoyed the challenges. I was determined to give the life a fair trial and I knew the novitiate wouldn't last long.' He also had a good relationship with his novice master and admired his common sense: 'When pressure built up, he would let us go bush for the day.'

The third brother, in his early thirties, experienced a culture shock on entering:

> Coming as I did from an era of the long-haired rebellious youth, a highly structured environment was more than I expected. Added to that, I was lonely, as my family were over two thousand miles away, and I was trying to work out why I was in religious life.

But he, too, had good things to say about the novitiate; he enjoyed the friendship of the brothers and appreciated the obvious concern of those in charge.

Structures and regimentation were certainly present in all brothers' novitiates. A brother in his sixties spoke for others when he said wryly:

> It would have been like a prison if we were compelled to stay—but we weren't. We knew we were well looked after. We were well fed, got good recreation and plenty of work. We were obliged to live up to a certain standard and accepted penances for all types of things. One penance was to have meals on our knees.

Brothers accepted, as did one in his forties,

> the quaint rituals such as silence at meals and using hand signs for things to be passed. They were part of the package deal. Other novices took everything for granted, so that restrained me from asking, 'What on earth is going on here?' If they took it for granted, then it must be normal.

Some things, as several brothers said, were absurd. The Office, for example, was said in Latin: 'It was total stupidity to be babbling this stuff that didn't make sense.' A few brothers were irritated by unnecessary detail: doors, for example, had to be left open to a particular angle. There was little emphasis on particular friendships and, when there was, it was not taken too seriously. A brother in his late thirties saw it as nonsense that he could not talk privately

with three fellow novices whom he had known since kinder-
garten days, so, as he said with a grin, 'You accepted the
dictates and learnt to get around the system.'

A forty-eight-year-old brother said: 'Most of our Irish
brothers were fairly Jansenistic, so it was pretty tough. But
that was the way they thought and we accepted it.' As
brothers mentioned points of irritation, they shrugged and
smiled: they had taken them with a grain of salt. I did not
detect anger or bitterness, except in one situation. After
joining a clerical congregation, brothers had discovered they
were completely segregated from those to be ordained. A
couple still felt a little resentful about this discrimination.

Three-quarters of the brothers explicitly stated that they
had enjoyed their novitiate. It was with fondness that all
these looked back to the novitiate. One said it was as if he
had been in a big family group and another even reported
that, for him, it had been a very relaxed period. Only one
novice master came in for flak. Others were very much
admired and liked. One brother said of his novice master: 'He
was really worthy of being our mate. He was a great
character.'

In comparison with sisters the changes introduced into
brothers' novitiates in the 1970s were relatively minor. A
brother in his early thirties remembered how his novice
master called in the community to explain changes he was
introducing into the novitiate. One big change was that
brothers were not asked to take religious names. Ironically,
this brother said the novices felt a bit deprived when they
later heard stories of the old brothers' novitiate: 'We felt we
weren't given a chance to prove our metal . . . we were treated
like human beings. We even had a fortnight's holiday and
four afternoons a week were free.' A thirty-year-old brother
said: 'Those in charge were obviously concerned for us. There
was certainly a sense of experimentation in formation but I
appreciated the fact that people were looking for the best
for us.'

In one novitiate it wasn't the novice master who introduced
change. A brother in his mid-thirties was one of twelve
novices who took change into their own hands:

The thing that struck me most was all this silence. Our group was rebellious about it. As a conscientious person, I tried to keep silence, but in the end our group just abolished it. Then we gave up on accusing ourselves of faults. The novice master was quite perturbed, but he finally accepted the situation.

Of the brothers, 40 per cent commented favourably on their spiritual formation. A brother in his seventies said: 'We didn't get a great depth in theology and scripture, but it was solid stuff.' 'The spiritual side', remarked a brother in his forties, 'was life-giving.' One brother in his forties claimed that, as a novice, he moved into spiritual overdrive and aimed at becoming a saint as quickly as possible. He appeared to be the only one to take his spirituality scrupulously, and that did not last long.

The attrition rate of brothers is high compared with sisters. A brother in his mid-thirties said that fourteen from a group of thirty-nine left during the novitiate; since then a further twenty have left. This, he suggested, was fairly normal. A brother in his early thirties had entered with nine other boys; three had been professed and two were still in religion. While sisters often feared they would be sent from the novitiate, brothers knew they could be and, according to one in his fifties, were frequently sent home. As another brother said: 'I never got close to anybody in the novitiate because the casualty rate was a little too high. You never knew when you might be sent home.'

Priests

The period of postulancy for priests varied from three years for one to the case of another whose congregation sent their candidates immediately to the novitiate, which usually consisted of one year, sometimes two. Priests were more vocal than brothers when they discussed the novitiate and their reactions were similar to those of sisters.

The contemplative priest began his novitiate very enthusiastically. His timetable was very rigid: 2.45 a.m. rising, with prayers until breakfast at 7 a.m.; work on the farm or in the house followed with prayers before dinner at

11 a.m.; prayers, a short siesta sometimes, two hours of work and spiritual reading filled in time before prayers and tea at 5 p.m. Novices then had spiritual reading again or were given a talk by the novice master before they joined the community for the superior's talk and night prayers. They were in bed by 8 p.m. Up to the 1960s there was no formal recreation, and silence was always observed. During his novitiate ten out of twelve novices left. He found this very unsettling and continually asked himself: 'Why don't I leave now? It's obviously going to happen sooner or later.'

The departure of novices did not worry everyone. A priest in his sixties explained his attitude:

> It was just like my old job situation. If people didn't like the conditions, they left. Whether I was happy or not depended on whether I could adjust to the conditions, so it was very much an individual choice.

Most priests found strict structures and the ensuing discipline a problem: 'They bugged me,' commented one, 'but intellectually I knew they were good for me.' Another priest found his seven-day programme with no free time difficult: 'It was the hardest year of my life. I survived on will power. However, I was utterly convinced that this was what my life was for. The novitiate was a necessary step.' Many agreed with him. Only one man in his sixties actually said he hated his novitiate, although he appeared to have accepted it philosophically. What he found most difficult was the hour's meditation night and morning: 'We weren't told how to pray or what prayer was. I kept listening to the chapel clock ticking over the minutes.'

For a number the novitiate was an anti-intellectual period. A priest in his sixties 'vegetated through the novitiate', but he willingly acknowledged the compensations: 'Although the process was hopeless, the vision was first class. We all knew what we were on about; we knew what we were going to do and we knew why.' Not all expectations were met. A priest in his fifties said: 'There was an emphasis on work and I began to realise there wasn't as much time for prayer as I'd thought.' Having worked for years before entering, a priest in his thirties saw his study as idleness: 'I felt I had gone out of a working environment into a lazy one.' A few others also felt that they were marking time. Not one priest complained of too much work.

In contrast with the brothers, the majority of priests, as well as sisters, spoke more about their emotions. Four spoke about feeling at home immediately they entered the novitiate. This feeling had little to do with the structures and expectations of the novitiate, but as one in his fifties said: 'I was just happy to go along with anything, and that included taking the discipline, fasting and wearing sandals in winter. I was happy because I was at home.'

A priest in his late thirties recalled his feelings of numbness. He had an emotional sense of being surrounded with high walls. Together with another priest in his late twenties, he found it difficult to cope with living closely with strangers without the family atmosphere of understanding and sympathy. Others mentioned feelings of loneliness and homesickness. After his family had left for home, a priest now in his forties remembered going to his room: 'I happened to catch a glimpse of myself in a mirror and I burst into tears. I suddenly realised what I had done. But that feeling didn't last long.'

After coming from a job where he had been accustomed to using his initiative, a priest in his thirties experienced a 'feeling of helplessness' when he entered. He said: 'I found it a bit peculiar that you were told how you were to work and for how long. They even instructed me how to ring the call bell.' One priest deliberately avoided frustration by resolutely avoiding judgmental thinking about what he was told to do.

Some priests found the various public corrections and penances ridiculous and upsetting, but as one in his sixties said: 'After a while you got accustomed to the fuss made over a trivial accident of smashing a cup.' A priest in his thirties recalled: 'You had to rake the grass whether there was anything there to rake or not.' A man in his fifties missed not being able to read newspapers and listen to the radio: 'I didn't see much sense in a lot of things,' he remarked, 'but I put up with the crazy ideas.'

Most priests had been in novitiates with relatively few

novices. Possibly the lack of numbers excluded the possibility of the physical sports brothers enjoyed, because only one priest emphasised sports as a feature of the novitiate. Several, however, enjoyed the walks they took as a group. A priest in his fifties remembered such walks: 'Thirty-two of us would set out together in full cassocks, sash and hat and all in black.' When novices were few, they usually formed part of a community of professed monks. One young priest said: 'This closeness with the community gave me a much deeper feel of what fraternity is all about.' The priests in large novitiates were the ones who spoke glowingly about the companionship they had experienced and how they had felt caught up in the spirit of the congregation. One had twenty-nine fellow novices: 'It was wonderful to pray and recreate together. My richest experience has been the novitiate year, because I knew on the deepest level what it meant to be a member of the congregation.' Two priests only referred to the ban on particular friendships: 'Touching one another', one said, 'was strictly forbidden.' The priests appreciated their novice masters: open, friendly, kind, commonsense and prayerful were common adjectives used in their description.

From their novitiate the men moved into the scholasticate or seminary, where they studied for six or seven years for ordination. This was a freer life. 'Not so much a pressure-cooker program' as a priest in his thirties commented. They assumed more responsibility, for example, some set their own prayer timetable. They were usually encouraged to use their initiative, especially with the pastoral work that was included in their programme. A priest in his fifties said: 'There was a completely different mentality in the scholasticate, and there was a good mixture of contemplation, community life, academic life and a great opportunity for sports.' Once ordained, the priests usually moved immediately into pastoral work in the parishes.

Conclusion

Both priests and sisters, especially the latter, appear to have found their novitiate more traumatic than did the brothers. After the novitiate the pressures certainly lifted from sisters, but their community life and the expectations of superiors, peers and laity perpetuated the sub-culture learnt in the novitiate. This was not so for priests. After the seminary's different conditioning — and six priests broadened their outlook as they studied overseas — their ministry of necessity brought them into contact with adults in family situations, and they lived in communities of two or three with greater freedom and responsibility. A priest in his fifties succinctly summed up the situation: 'The idea was to toe the line in the novitiate and, as soon as you were out, you threw it [sub-culture] all off.' This is what sisters, mostly living a semi-enclosed life style, were unable to do. It is also interesting to note that, when brothers and priests referred to a member of their congregation, they often used, not the title, 'brother' or 'father', but 'man'. In not one case did sisters refer to a companion as 'woman': 'it was always 'sister'.

Vows: chastity, poverty, obedience 4

*T*he basic form of religious profession is similar in male and female congregations: the members, in the name of Jesus Christ, make to God the simple vows of chastity, poverty and obedience according to the constitutions of their particular congregation. The profession is a public and formal promise to live the religious life, and the vows are the means for doing this. By the first vow the members bind themselves to observe celibacy and to abstain from every act contrary to it. By the simple vow of poverty, members renounce the right to dispose of any temporal thing without the permission of the proper superior. The vow of obedience binds them to obey precepts of a lawful superior in those things that belong directly or indirectly to the life of the congregation, that is, the observance of the vows and the constitutions or rule of life.

Chastity

Sisters

The brevity with which the vow of chastity was dismissed in early constitutions is indicative of the awe, silence and fear that surrounded it. Sisters were bound by this vow to what was sometimes termed the practice of 'the angelic virtue'. No one explained how angels without bodies and so without sexual urges and human beings with normal, functioning bodies could have 'the angelic virtue' in common. Sisters could openly admit to breaches of the vows of poverty and obedience and ask for guidance in these areas. It was unthinkable to fail in the vow of chastity. Guidance in this area was therefore not required.

Unrecognised affective energy was channelled into compulsive work. Although homosexuality was not named, friendships were discouraged and dismissed as 'particular' and therefore dangerous. The semi-enclosure of the majority of sisters effectively locked out anything other than brief and business-like contact with men. Until the 1970s a sister in some congregations would have a companion with her when she visited her doctor: this practice symbolised how the

Catholic Church saw the fragility of feminine virginity and male aggressiveness. Two other factors can be noted. Nine sisters, two below the age of forty, firmly believe that they would have remained single had they not entered. Ten out of thirteen Irish sisters have experienced no difficulty with celibacy. As a fifty-year-old Irish sister explained: 'Perhaps it has something to do with our culture, but I don't believe Irish women have much difficulty with celibacy. My friends and I haven't.' Thirty-six out of the hundred sisters interviewed entered their congregations immediately after the completion of their schooling; twenty-five were Australian girls, and eleven were Irish. Fifteen of the thirty-six entered directly from boarding schools or juniorates. These women, therefore, had little or no opportunity to mingle socially with men before they joined their congregations.

The older sisters in this study dismissed the topic of chastity summarily. Seventeen of the twenty-three sisters over sixty-five years of age specifically stated that they had never experienced a problem with this vow. From their replies it would seem that they were so accepting of virginity as a state for themselves that it was virtually impossible for them to transgress it. They had grown up in an era when sexual matters were not openly discussed, and women were not expected to take pleasure in genital relationships. Many sisters admitted that they had been very ignorant, some even after they had made profession of their vows. A certain romanticism resulted. A seventy-seven-year-old sister said: 'I dedicated myself as a bride to Christ from my first holy communion, and I never went back on that.' Several agreed with a sister in her mid-seventies: 'I was never challenged in this vow.' One in her late seventies saw her only temptation against celibacy in a strong attachment to her family. Another was scrupulous in her early religious life: 'Dressing and bathing presented problems, but I couldn't talk about them to any one. I took the vow without knowing what I was giving up.'

A sister in her late sixties had witnessed or heard about so many problems in marriages that she was grateful for her celibate state. Few sisters in this age-group said that they had developed good friendships. One seventy-three-year-old sister explained: 'As soon as you began a friendly relationship with a sister in the community, they would move you. As long as you were not getting on well together, they would leave you there.' The effects of such attitudes are present today according to a forty-four-year-old superior:

> The older sisters don't relate very well to each other, so they are lonely. They want the younger ones to stay home more to talk to them, listen to them and entertain them. I find it very sad that they can't talk to each other on any but a superficial level.

Cultural changes in attitudes towards women and sexuality, together with new ministries involving sisters in a wider world than that of school and hospital, have gradually brought a new dimension to the vow of chastity. The majority of sisters between fifty and sixty-five years were able to talk more comfortably about their vow and what it has meant to them. On the whole, this group were able to assess objectively the effects on themselves of earlier attitudes. A fifty-nine-year-old sister commented: 'Authority made us cope with chastity by tiring us out and working us to capacity while frowning upon any friendship between two sisters. It caused a rigidity and lovelessness in our lives.'

A sixty-year-old sister recalled:

> As novices we were told never to touch a child or we would endanger our chastity. Yet it is the most normal thing to hug and reassure children if they fall over. The only real difficulty people have with chastity is when they allow fear to dry up love in their hearts.

Those who were warm and affectionate by nature learnt as young religious to maintain a guard when relating to people. Some, like a sixty-six-year-old sister, still deliberately distance themselves if people try to come close to them. Others have been able to shed earlier inhibitions. A sixty-two-year-old sister said:

> When I was a young religious it was instilled into me that the worst thing that could possibly happen was to lose my virginity. Even to have temptations against chastity was very bad. Today, I don't believe that. I can accept I'm human and I can let myself

love people where I felt before I could not, in case I might be tempted.

Several sisters in their fifties remember their horror when they experienced sexual feelings: 'Everything in that area', explained one, 'was considered a mortal sin.' Most sisters in this age-group now look at chastity more realistically. A few have developed close, not physical, relationships with men. One sixty-three-year-old was in her early fifties when she first met a man to whom she was very attracted.

> It was a turning-point in my life, because I really did love him. He wanted to marry me, and we talked about it a lot. His love for me taught me what true love was; I could understand for the first time the Lord's love for me. I had to decide whether to stay in religious life or marry him. I finally realised that the Lord had first priority in my life. I realised the value of religious life for me.

An understanding of and appreciation for chastity were often won from challenges to it. This was most frequently the case for sisters under fifty years. Three sisters in the study had experienced a lesbian relationship, two for a short period, the third for three years. This last sister, aged thirty-nine, had begun the relationship at a period when she was feeling very insecure and unhappy about the rapid changes in religious life; and she had terminated it seven years ago.

> I finally knew I would have to leave the congregation if I didn't end it, because I felt integrity was lacking. In a sense, then, I chose my religious vocation a second time, and it was definitely God who helped me. The sister involved and I are still good friends, and I value her friendship. In one way I am sorry it happened, because it was wrong. In another way I am not sorry. We fall in the mud, but I know now that God is there with us. I have learnt more about God and his love for me.

It was in the early 1970s that a far greater number of sisters began studying overseas or out of their convent environment in Australia. Spiritual courses involving religious men and women more than lay people often meant that, for the first time, religious men and women came into close contact for a considerable length of time, sometimes a year. It was inevitable that many formed friendships which resulted in some leaving the religious life to marry and others making a second and more responsible choice for religious life. From their experience the latter had a greater knowledge of what they were surrendering and a greater appreciation of the life they chose. The story of a forty-four-year-old sister is typical of sisters in her situation. She fell in love with a religious brother and the attraction was mutual.

It was a beautiful experience for me: it has been an experience of deeper commitment and tremendous support in that commitment. We talked frankly about how we felt. It was like meeting my other half. I was very much at home with him. I know that I am totally accepted as I am and he knows everything about me. I can accept myself, because he has accepted me. When I feel I am rejected by others, I don't unduly worry now. The love we have for each other has taught me so much about God and prayer. It made me realise that on earth one can never hold God: there can only be a yearning to do so. That helped me accept the absence of a physical relationship with this man.

A sister in her early forties had become involved with a priest when she was in her early thirties. It was a crisis in her life. She said:

I moved out of the situation, because I couldn't look at it clearly while I was so close to him. I talked it through with an objective person and finally cut my ties with the priest. That relationship had many good consequences. It put me in touch with the gift of being a woman. I learnt a lot about myself and relationships. It made me stop and look seriously at my call to religious life. It was a turning-point: I re-committed myself to religious life in a very special way.

Another group of sisters found that when they had no companionship or understanding within the religious community they mingled more with lay people, as they were able to do in the 1970s. For example, when she was in her thirties, a forty-six-year-old sister found herself in a community with women much older than herself. Having little in common with them, she sought friendship with lay men and women: 'I found I could share a lot with them, and it was exciting for me. I had a very wise provincial superior at that time who knew of my friendships and with whom I could be very open.'

By the late 1970s most sisters were wearing clothes similar to or identical with those worn by lay women, and they commented that this change in dress played an important part in the growing ease in relationships between themselves and the laity. It also played an equally important part in helping the sister to appreciate herself as an individual and as a woman.

Sisters under forty-five years of age were articulate in their explanation of the meaning of the vow of chastity for themselves. They have a great appreciation of its positive advantages. A forty-four-year-old sister said: 'Chastity is my favourite, most joyful vow. It gives me a freedom to relate to others; I don't own anyone and no one owns me. The vow emphasises the dignity of each human being.' Freedom to relate to others without possessiveness was mentioned by others. This is what a thirty-six-year-old sister had to say:

I have often thought I would be stifled in a marriage that would not allow me to reach out to all the people I now can. That's a very positive side to chastity for me. Chastity is also a stand against what society values: with my chastity I am saying that one can have important and valuable relationships with men without necessarily a genital relationship. I'm only missing out on one aspect of relationship, and I feel everything I am gaining far outweighs what society says I have lost.

There was no doubt that this renunciation of genital relationship results in suffering. For a thirty-seven-year-old sister, pain or suffering had for long been seen as a punishment. She explained her present attitude:

I came to realise that pain or suffering is a normal part of life. It has a lot to do with learning a new skill or a new way of behaving—like learning to ride a bicycle. It is always painful to learn and grow through the awkwardness of a yet unacquired skill. I have come to see the pain of celibacy in this way: I have to face the loss of never belonging to a husband, never bearing a

51

child, and then to learn another way of life. This learning will be painful.

Squarely facing the same natural urges, a thirty-nine-year-old sister counted her gains and knows what she wants in life. She realises a choice of any particular way of life necessarily excludes options for another:

> In the last couple of years I have been much more conscious of sexual stirrings within me. I have longings for intimacy, for a relationship that would be a relief from the solitude of living alone. I am more in touch with myself as a woman and a person, knowing I am capable of tenderness and wanting to be tender in a relationship with a man. I have met a couple of men to whom I was attracted, but when it came to the crunch, the value of a relationship within marriage did not really challenge the values I see in the life I live now.

Older sisters tended to view their vow of chastity as essential and a means for admittance to the religious life. They were encouraged to build excessive safeguards around it. It was then best forgotten. For younger sisters the vow of chastity is more than a vow whereby they can be admitted to a religious congregation. It is first and foremost a commitment to a relationship with God, a commitment to a specific way of relating to God, which they see as incompatible with marriage. Hence they choose chastity. Because they recognise the human need for companionship and support of fellow beings, they join a religious congregation in order to become a member of a community of like-minded individuals. A thirty-one-year-old sister summed up the attitude of many young sisters:

> In my struggle with the vow of chastity I realised I was basically selfish. Chastity is the challenge not to be selfish. In community I found I was almost expecting others to live in terms of me. Often we think we are loving people, whereas in fact we are loving ourselves in the way we relate to them. We subtly manoeuvre the situation to our own advantage. So, for me, chastity is a purifying of relationships so that the other becomes more the centre.
>
> In marriage I think I would have become too involved with one person. When I chose chastity in religious life, I chose to live a

kind of mad faith that says God is enough. Chastity is very much part of my relationship with God—for this reason I had chosen the single state before I chose religious life. I entered religious life because I felt community life is important for me. It is a check on me, a dreamer. If you live alone, you can very easily fool yourself.

Brothers

Eight brothers experience the vow of chastity as a problem with varying degrees of intensity. The majority find it does not bother them: two claim that temperamentally they would shun one-to-one relationships, even as laymen. They get on well with individuals, but as one said: 'I always draw a line at a certain point.' The second pointed out a factor applicable to most brothers:

> The conditioning we went through as young men taught us not to look for emotional satisfaction from others, and it has left me feeling a bit inadequate when it comes to emotional encounters with people. And that's probably a good thing.

Implicitly or explicitly, most brothers agreed with the remark of one in his seventies: 'For two-thirds of my religious life we were taught to look at chastity negatively. Chastity was seen as a forty-foot pole keeping people, especially women, at a distance.' A brother in his forties said all in his congregation had been warned 'to steer off contact with women, especially those on the teaching staff, so I became very fearful of any communication with them'. It was very much a macho ideal presented. 'Toughness, an absence of softness and sensitivity', explained a brother, 'were all part of the male model we had to aim at if we were to be manly.'

The vow of chastity, according to a brother in his mid-thirties, is necessary for community living, and community is necessary for ministry.

> For this purpose [he continued], the development of the individual is ensured, and his relationship with Christ and the community members fostered. Primarily I see this vow as one allowing me to join a community, so that in relating to others I don't have to worry about how it will affect my relationship with one particular

person, as I would if I were married. I'm free to be available to all people.

He wondered, therefore, about the viability of newly formed communities consisting of married couples and religious: 'I wouldn't know what is seen as the priority in their commitment — to one another or to the group as a whole.' In his opinion such a radical variation from the norm will not survive.

Relationship with men and women is now acceptable and sometimes encouraged among brothers. Long accustomed to the forty-foot pole ideal, some older brothers slowly learnt to relate more comfortably with women, usually sisters, during long renewal courses. A brother in his sixties found new friendships formed during a live-in course very rewarding: 'The fact I was a brother associating with sisters meant we felt safe with each other. We knew the boundaries and respected them. I genuinely grew to love them, and that love has remained.' A younger brother commented: 'Years ago you wouldn't dream of going out to dinner with a woman, but today it's left to your own responsible decision.' Another brother said:

At last I have become more comfortable with myself as a religious, loving people and letting them know I care for them. I have some very close, wholesome friendships with women. There's now a far healthier atmosphere surrounding our friendships.

With greater freedom came inevitable problems. During the course of his work, one brother in his late thirties was sometimes away from his community for a weekend and was with Catholic laymen. At first he was astounded at their assumptions, but has learnt to cope with them. He spoke about one incident:

This guy said to me, 'I don't know how you feel, but if you want a bird tonight, no worries. I've got one for you.' Now he was obviously just trying to be helpful, but other guys who would be delighted to pull down the church make these offers.

Most brothers who admitted difficulties with the vow of chastity said it was not so much the absence of genital relationships that was the cause. They long for the companionship of one particular person, and they miss the warmth and joy of a family. 'I would dearly love to have someone close to me,' said a brother in his thirties. One confessed: 'I have a passionate love for children. I almost go demented when I see a baby.' Another brother in his early forties reported:

Chastity has become harder. I was full of enthusiasm and dedication in my twenties and early thirties. Now I look at people about forty who have growing families and I feel I've missed out on that aspect of life. It begins to eat away at you. It's more a conscious lack of one's own family group rather than a hankering for a sexual relationship.

A man in his fifties consoles himself for not having children by remembering the difficulties of rearing them. Another brother in his mid-thirties does not think in terms of marriage for himself, but he enjoys taking his nieces and nephews out for the day. There was wistfulness in his comment: 'I look around at them and they all have fair hair like mine so I feel like their Dad.'

When they do not find compatible company within their community or are experiencing serious personal problems, religious men and women are very vulnerable. One brother told his story:

I've done about six back somersaults along the way. Some years back I was trying to build up my spiritual life and deepen my prayer when the doctors diagnosed an illness that could have been terminal. This girl I knew was very understanding and supportive. We had sex before I went into hospital, and all fears left me. Later I wondered how this could have happened at a time I was very serious about my relationship with the Lord. It seemed to me he was saying, 'If you want to know what love is then you have to experience it in a physical way.' My commitment to religious life strengthened and we broke off the relationship.

Within his family a brother had found it natural to express his affections by physical touch: 'It was acceptable for males to hug and kiss one another.' He had taken up yoga and became, as he said, more attuned to his body and senses. Hence community for him was cold and isolating. When he was experiencing strong urges to have a sexual relationship with a woman, in desperation he asked a brother had he ever felt such urges. 'He was reading a paper. He didn't even look up. He just said "No", and I was left hanging there.' Lack of understanding and sympathy finally led him to spend time talking to a woman who was experiencing difficulties within her marriage. 'Gradually we began giving each other a kiss and a hug. It was my first experience of falling in love. I didn't deliberately set out to have sex with her but that's what happened.' It was not to be his only affair.

> Finally [he said], I realised I had to stop a kind of continuous sex life. It would have been dishonest to continue, and I would have soon lost the sense of my religious vocation and left. I worked it out that, if I left for the wrong reasons, I'd still have my own problems and it wouldn't be fair to my wife and possibly the kids. I had to come to terms with important questions. First, to choose to love women and not to react against them because of my relationship with them. I had to accept responsibility for myself and my own actions and not blame others. Second, I had to accept that my whole cultural background and temperament led me to express my affections in some physical way, and I had to learn not to go further than a brief touch or hug. I see celibacy now as the marriage between God and myself.

These two brothers learnt valuable lessons from their intimate relationships with women. They did not mention whether the women were as fortunate.

Priests

While admitting some difficulties with their vow of chastity, mainly in the years between thirty-five and forty-five, older priests did not elaborate on them. Three priests, all in their fifties, stated that they have not been worried by this vow. Priests under fifty said their vow of chastity was the most difficult for them. The latter, with three exceptions, recognise that chastity creates a vacuum in their lives and are active in their efforts to find compensation. One in his mid-forties explained:

> Sexuality is such a basic drive and need in our lives that unless religious life, through prayer and community living, is rich and full, then a whole dimension of our life is missing. I have to work hard at religious life to compensate for what I miss out on.

Ten years younger, another priest who is presently struggling with his vow of chastity realises the truth of this statement in his own life: 'I really don't have a basic problem with any particular vow. I have a problem with community life. It's not working for me at the moment so I'm having trouble with my vow of chastity.' Younger priests echo the words of a thirty-four-year-old: 'Religious life needs to be fully lived through prayer and community life to realise and achieve what I've surrendered through my vow of chastity.'

More than brothers and priests in other fields, priests in parishes come into contact with women. For young priests, fresh from the enclosure of a seminary, this can lead to them coming to grips with their sexual drive for the first time. As one in his mid-thirties said:

> It's a mystery to me how I've suppressed my sexual instincts over the past years. I think it has to do with being buried in work, with finding escape in such physical activities as football. I was also in schools and so was at a distance from women and that is one way of repressing sexual feeling.

Recently moved from school to parish ministry, another priest said:

> I was regularly visiting a number of women I liked. It took me quite a while to unearth my motivation, which was a sexual enjoyment and a feeling of intimacy with them. There wasn't anything subterranean going on. I just felt relaxed and happy with them, and I was able to talk about myself. I've reached the stage where I can say my vision of heaven is sitting down with a female friend and a glass of wine.

Presently involved in a relationship with a woman, a priest in his thirties is battling with his vocation. His comments reveal how closely for him the vow is tied up with other issues:

I don't know whether I'll decide to stay or leave. I did not come into the congregation by mistake, so I have a sense of a pattern in my life and a loyalty to the congregation. Yet changes in religious life have affected me. We used to have between twenty-five and thirty novices, now we're lucky to have two. People are no longer interested in the church and they see religious as having nothing to offer them; some even see religious life as an impediment to adult maturity. Yet the world doesn't appeal to me. As I see it, the question for me is one of conversion, and I don't want it yet. If I was sincere, I'd be praying about it, but I'm too frightened to pray.

On the whole, younger priests look on chastity positively and realistically. For most, chastity only makes sense because it frees them to be of service to people. As one priest remarked: 'That is a practical concept, but this loneliness we experience as humans is also part of the cross of Jesus.' Another priest said: 'Chastity has made me more aware of people. It is liberating because I can be with people without possessiveness or limited by a commitment to a particular family group.'

Not everyone sees the vow of chastity as eliminating close relationships. A priest in his forties, enjoying close friendship with a few men and women, said: 'Chastity is incompatible with genital intimacy, but not with the intimacy of close relationships, for this is an essential part of a celibate life.' He spoke for most priests when he added: 'I do find celibacy a struggle, and I'm glad I do, because otherwise I wouldn't be normal.' His would be the sane, common-sense attitude towards the vow of chastity that most religious interviewed in this study expressed.

Poverty

Sisters

To the late 1960s and beyond, in some congregations, there

was no difficulty for the sisters in the interpretation or living out of their vow of poverty: they could not make one decision regarding it. Even the number of stockings and handkerchiefs was prescribed. In some congregations, clothes were circulated. What one sister wore one month was given to another the following month. Whenever they needed something even as essential and small as a toothbrush, they asked permission from the superior to obtain it from the bursar or from a cupboard in which supplies were stored. Once they had taken the vow of poverty, they had no further responsibility but to rely on the superior for their needs. It was practically impossible in those circumstances to have more than the minimum of possessions, and those they had were usually not called, for example, 'my veil' but 'the veil'. Moreover, the sisters in the 1960s had either lived through the depression years as religious or were children of parents who had done so. Therefore, as most sisters or their parents had experienced real poverty, the word 'poverty' had a clear meaning for them.

Today, however, the greater percentage of sisters in this study, including those over eighty years, are uncomfortable when they talk about the vow of poverty. 'It is difficult to interpret,' they say. 'I haven't an answer to what it means, so I don't think about it much.' Or, 'I am very confused about the vow of poverty. Everyone in the community seems to have a different idea about it.' The replies may vary, but the message is the same. Sisters are concerned about the interpretation of the word 'poverty' in their lives. It no longer means what it once did. What they believe it now enshrines for them is at variance with their old interpretation and that of lay people. The result is uncertainty. As so many said to me: 'I am very uncomfortable about this vow of poverty.' Many factors, other than Vatican II documents, have contributed to this uncertainty. The following have emerged from this study.

The sub-culture of religious life has gradually disintegrated over the last twenty years. While sisters in a few congregations had always lived in groups of two or three close to lay people and had depended very much on their material support, many sisters were in larger communities, involved in institutional works of school and hospital. When the latter began moving out from institutions and coming more into contact with what they once called 'the world', they saw at first hand the conditions of the materially poor, and the contrast with what they called 'poverty' was great. Always they had shelter, food, clothing and security. They even had a high status among those with whom they came in contact: the poor of the world did not. And the understanding of the word 'poverty' by these poor forced sisters to re-examine the meaning of the word for themselves.

Once their enclosure regulations were eased and then discarded, sisters also came to appreciate that they were not the only ones committed to good works; the laity, too, wanted to follow the ideals of the Gospel. Where the world had been seen as a threat to religious life, a place where vocations to religious life were lost, it gradually became recognised as something good in itself. People came to be seen and liked as individuals, no longer simply as souls to be won and harvested for heaven. Sisters gained a greater respect and love for the creation of God. One of the first points to emerge from the interviews was that some sisters no longer believe that the taking of three vows is important and part of a profession to the religious life. Not all are putting this belief into so many words. They use words similar to those of a fifty-year-old sister: 'I rarely think about or refer to the vows. I used to, but not now. I can't see them, especially the vow of poverty, as having any great relevance in themselves or in my life.' What such sisters are saying, it seems to me, is that they no longer agree with the traditional definition of poverty. It is very evident that they are living out a new theology of religious life and have not yet discovered a better word than 'poverty' to describe it.

Poverty, according to a sister in her forties, has many connotations in society and culture: it is a term covering a range of degrees of material deprivation. Sisters all agree that their life cannot be described as one of material poverty. This disturbs a few who want a return to the traditional living out of poverty. A seventy-three-year-old sister is worried: 'I don't feel the pinch of poverty, so I wonder if I am keeping my vow.' An eighty-year-old sister deplores the fact that religious are no longer keeping the vow of poverty. Such sisters struggle amid what they see as affluent circumstances to keep their vow as they were taught to do fifty years ago. Only two other sisters would agree with the few older ones that they should be experiencing material poverty. The first, thirty-six years old, said:

> I am coming more and more to see that we should be materially poor. I used to talk about simplicity of lifestyle but I think now that is a cop-out. I would find it almost impossible to live in some of our convents — the conditions there are so good.

She went on to say: 'We religious are associated with the powerful in our society. To me that is not poverty. I have to learn what it means to be poor if I am going to be true even to the church's call to live justly today.' Basically, she is saying she wants to associate herself with the powerless, the unjustly treated, and she sees the only way of doing this is to become materially poor. Others, as will be seen later, would agree with her objective, but not with her means. The second sister, thirty-one years old, said:

> I cannot conceive of being a religious, of being caught up in God without the vow of poverty that means all the dimensions of poverty. I have to be ready to accept my own poverty of self and that of those with whom I live. I have to accept that they can't do what I would like them to do, or even what they would like to do. Poverty also means being very much in solidarity with the materially poor. If religious are not actually poor, their life becomes almost invalid, especially in a materialistic, capitalistic society. For religious life to be authentic, to have any meaning at all today, we have to show where we stand. As long as religious life is wishy-washy, it has no future.

Some sisters directly spoke of poverty as being evil, something to be avoided and to be eradicated. 'Reducing ourselves to the level of the materially poor', commented a sister in her fifties, 'doesn't necessarily do much to foster freedom either in ourselves or in others.' Another sister in her mid-thirties said: 'Earlier I thought we had to look like people on skid row. I don't think so now.' Most tried to include the word 'poverty' when they described their lifestyle; they spoke also about 'poverty of spirit'. One explained: 'Poverty of spirit locks in very deeply with my dependence on God. It expresses more my faith than my physical living. It is not tangible.'

The following are extracts from several sisters' comments on poverty. Their age is indicated at the end of each extract.

I see it as a vow that embraces the spiritual dimension of our lives. It is a very important vow, as it means accepting the poverty in our own spiritual life and in our own personalities as well. It is far more embracing than I saw it in the past and in every area more a vow of detachment. (63 years)

Poverty means to be able to abandon completely all I love in a community and in my work and move on at the direction of my congregation. Leaving the people I come to love and leaving the work I have built up—that has been my hardest poverty. (57 years)

The real basis of my vow is the deep acceptance that I, as a human person, a creature, am totally dependent on the Creator. (47 years)

For me poverty is an openness to share my own personal resources, my intellect, skills, time, energies, and, I guess, my feelings with others. I should share the resources to which I have access—including those of my congregation. (35 years)

I don't see the vow of poverty in terms of things. It is not so much what we have, but our attitude to them: possessions should not possess us. A religious should be available to others, flexible in her activities and movements, a person who does not get caught up in positions and promotions and who realises that, ultimately, her life rests on God's providence. (25 years)

The majority of sisters interviewed would concur with the above statements. This is not to say that they ignore the material aspect of poverty. Sisters are now well aware of the wealth that most of their congregations possess in land and buildings and sometimes in investments. Some are choosing to move out from administrative positions in their congregational institutions of school and hospital, but they are doing so with an awareness of their responsibility to the corporate body and of that body's responsibility to the people serviced by the institution. Only when suitable lay people can replace them do they relinquish their positions of control.

Sisters emphasised simplicity of lifestyle, a lifestyle akin to that of the ordinary person. This was their most common statement. They want to be ordinary people and be seen as such. Some make a definitive choice. As a sister in her forties pointed out: 'I would very much like a holiday at Ayers Rock, but so would others who live in my area. No way could they afford to go, so neither should I.' Others, for example a sixty-three-year-old sister, accept gratefully whatever is given, whether it is less of what they want or a trip overseas. Sisters are emphasising the importance of continually checking on one's attitude to possessions: 'How free am I to let them go when I really don't need them?' This attitude, together with a personal money allowance, has helped sisters to have a respect and responsibility for material goods. They believe they should be seen to take a stand against consumerism by living a simple lifestyle in keeping with their neighbours. Within communities, however, there is a wide spectrum of inter-pretation of the vow of poverty, and this often causes tension. A forty-two-year-old sister believes that, because sisters come from different economic backgrounds, they cannot even share a completely common view of poverty. Perhaps, as another sister in her forties suggests, tension over poverty will exist until the community is open and trusting enough to talk as a group about their views. Only three sisters interviewed felt that their communities were able so to talk.

Sisters are sufficiently realistic to acknowledge that, although they might live as poorly as a poor family, they can never be poor in reality: basically, they choose to live as they do, whereas the poor have no choice. As a forty-nine-year-old sister said: 'If I buy books, there won't be less food on the table.' A sister in her late thirties has the same opinion: 'I will never be really poor, because I have one thing that lifts me above poverty and that is education. I can always get a job.' Other sisters, however, would not agree with her. It has become increasingly difficult for sisters, especially those over fifty years of age, to secure jobs even within the Catholic education system. Preference seems to be given to younger lay teachers. The congregation, however, provides a financial security that the poor cannot experience. Most sisters see this security as a positive good: because they are members of a large group sharing their resources, they are therefore able to place their advantages, for example, education, skills in communication, counselling techniques, at the service of the poor. There are a minority of sisters doing this in new ways in poor suburbs. They live in what they call 'an open house'; that is, they welcome anyone who wants to come and chat with them. They feel that they are saying: 'We are on your side. That is why we choose to live here.' Where possible, they help the poor in their individual needs. One fifty-seven-year-old sister is more actively involved on a community level: she is working to improve the general rather than the individual lot of the poor. She is thus publicly acknowledging that material poverty should be eradicated and that she herself is actively on the side of the powerless in their struggle against the powerful. This is a far cry from the interpretation of the vow of poverty some fifty, even twenty, years ago.

Brothers

A brother in his sixties confessed: 'Poverty has got me worried at present. I am not sure of the right answers to it.' He, with a few others, believes that religious on the whole have drifted away from what he sees as the ideal of a simple lifestyle, and he deplores the lack of witness to the value of poverty. For them, and indeed for all the brothers interviewed, poverty is not an end in itself. As one said:

> Doing without material things helps us realise it is God working through us. Poverty leads us to depend on God instead of seeing ourselves as powerful and efficient. I reckon using money a bit carelessly will destroy something of the meaning of being religious.

The majority of brothers, however, are not overly concerned about the material aspect of the vow of poverty. For them it is not a big issue. A brother in his fifties summed up their attitude:

Poverty never worries me. As far as money and possessions go, well, they don't belong to me and I haven't any attachment to them. If I need to use something and it's there, I use it. If it's not there, and it's not essential to my work, I do without it. No fuss.

Some brothers commented that, in their opinion, their communities as groups and/or some particular brothers were living too affluently. They, however, could do nothing about the situation and aimed to live as simply as possible on a personal level. Several deliberately keep their own expenditure to that of a man in a struggling family situation.

A brother in his early forties spoke for several when he said he thinks of poverty in terms of his contribution as a person — his time, talents, knowledge — to those for whom he works. Others emphasised the responsibility to be careful with money and things. Overall, on a very practical level, brothers take it for granted they should — and they do — live a simple lifestyle. Their personal possessions are few. As one brother said: 'I travel light.' They have a practical outlook. One superior was not worried that brothers occasionally 'put a few bob on the horses'. When he first became superior, he realised that the brothers' incidental money had previously been inadequate, with the result they were constantly anxious lest they have insufficient funds for necessary expenses. To relieve them of their anxiety and to encourage personal responsibility for wise expenditure, he told the bursar to give the brothers whatever money they requested. He said:

We nearly went broke for six months or so. Then, when the brothers realised they could get what they needed when they needed it, they settled down and the demand dwindled. As a community, we now work out where we can economise in order to give a bit extra to poor families we know.

Three brothers live within communities that have decided, as a group, to live more simply and economically. In one community they now cook, clean and do their own laundry, and they distribute the money thus saved among poor families. From a similar economy, a second community pays school fees for two poor families: 'This does mean we miss out on some things for ourselves', explained a brother, 'and we're happy about that.'

Contrast between what they envisage as in keeping with a religious vow of poverty and what their ministry requires or permits creates conflict and confusion, especially for those managing large businesses, in most cases schools. Two brothers in this situation have the personal use of a car. They expressed concern that an independent use of a car outside business requirements affected the spirit of poverty and one added another aspect: 'If I get sick of the community, I am easily able to get away in the car, so I haven't always stayed to confront some issues.' A brother in his late forties acknowledged that in continually using expensive equipment to facilitate his work—and he knows that to do so is now essential—he has lost sight of material poverty. Because he works under great pressure for long periods, he finds it imperative to have occasional complete breaks from his environment.

> I disappear for a couple of days. I usually book into a motel and just relax, completely away from the school and community. That is at variance with normal community living, but given my work pressures and my own temperament, I feel I must do this in order to continue working efficiently. I am comfortable with what I do, but uncomfortable that others may not understand why I am doing it and be scandalised.

Poverty for him, at this stage, he said, has become a case of living out an availability and a willingness to serve.

Background and external influences have also shaped the concept of poverty. For a brother in his mid-thirties poverty is a very important vow, because of the contrast between the attitude his struggling family had towards money and that of many brothers. Arriving at his present community, he had been shocked at what he judged as affluent circumstances and lifestyle. Religious, he strongly believed, should always witness to material poverty. Within his congregation, many share his views, and the issue of poverty has become a very sensitive area giving rise to heated discussions among the brothers. A brother in his forties also entertains similar views arising from his own family's necessary economy.

On the other hand, one brother in his forties has no qualms about his bank account: 'I have a fair bit of money backing me. Most is in investments and given by my family. If I want something I think is unfair for the community to supply, I mention it to my superior and use my own money.'

Driven by his own emotional suffering, another brother became involved with patients in a mental hospital. When the material poverty of many of them led him to initiate practical schemes to assist them, he became more aware of the importance of money and of using it productively and carefully. A fourth brother, in his thirties, was involved with ill and handicapped people and, so, for him,

> Poverty has nothing to do with money or material things. It is recognising and accepting my helplessness and complete dependence on God. I have to come to the realisation that I can't solve all the problems of the world. Religious can easily become smug and secure in what they are doing. As a group we have to confront what it actually means to be poor in spirit, and that is to divest ourselves of our own problems and inhibitions because these things prevent us from reaching out to people.

A brother in his late thirties gives little thought to personal material comfort. Poverty for him means working on his negative qualities. He gave an example:

> Anger can destroy. My anger can deprive me of personal worth—that is poverty for me. It can prevent my having a good relationship with the boys I teach. I work against this poverty by trying to develop my personal riches, my good qualities.

Priests

Although there were the expected variations in thinking, priests evinced no doubts about their interpretation of the vow of poverty. Admitting it was relative, they emphasised material poverty. As a group they aimed at a simple lifestyle with no extremes: they saw this as basic to the vow of poverty, so a common-sense outlook on poverty was held. A priest in his late fifties, for example, lives in an area where the temperature soars over forty degrees celsius for long periods. He said: 'I limit myself to one can of beer a day. There's the money for it, but I don't think I should buy more.' Another priest in his middle fifties lives in a wealthy suburb: 'I may have to walk out tomorrow and live elsewhere, but while I'm here, I'm going to enjoy the beautiful houses and gardens.' A priest in his late forties gave his opinion: 'Life's meant to be enjoyable with a sense of modest comfortableness. The most important thing a religious can do is model a good, happy, healthy way of living.'

A few priests felt some unease about the general living standards of religious. A sixty-year-old remarked: 'We reflect a middle class mentality in religious life . . . there is not much real poverty for us. Yet I wouldn't want us to live extremely poor lives—that to me would be barren living.' This group mentality worried some priests. 'Community life would be better', commented a thirty-five-year-old, 'if the members would talk together about a common and simple lifestyle.' A thirty-six-year-old priest would like religious to move out of large substantial monasteries: 'Poverty requires living with the poor of our society, and if we do that, then the simple life-style will automatically follow.' Several priests felt that the living standards of communities as such were too high. A priest in his sixties believes in a living standard comparable to that of the average person in whatever suburb or town he resides: 'Sometimes', he said, 'I am ashamed when people come to the presbytery because we have more than they have.' Two others spoke of similar embarrassment when they see families calculating if they can afford an evening's enter-tainment. As one said: 'We don't have the experience of having to tighten our belts, of having to restrict our plans because we need money for essentials such as food.' Viewing poverty more as a communal issue, three priests hold that religious were living too comfortably. One in his mid-thirties said: 'We're no longer what we say we are. We've become accustomed to cars, three meals a day and a roof over our heads . . . but we've also lost something.' These priests want a more radical lifestyle, but see it as impossible for them as individuals to live differently from the communities they are in: 'A radical common lifestyle', said one, 'would require a completely different attitude of heart and mind among the priests, and I don't see that happening.'

Acknowledging that it would be very difficult to alter expectations of the community with regard to lifestyle, most priests concentrated on individual responsibilities. One in his fifties commented on changes that have occurred in the individual's practice of poverty: 'We take it for granted now that, if we receive gifts, we keep them instead of handing them over to the superior.' The majority agreed that the individual religious today has a greater personal responsibility for his observance of the vow of poverty. A sixty-five-year-old priest spoke for the majority when he said: 'I try to live frugally with a minimum of demands on the common purse.' One in his fifties admitted his failure in another aspect of poverty: 'I'm well within my vow of poverty and I live a pretty simple lifestyle but I'm surrounded by clutter of clothes, books and notes. The call of the poor Christ is to get rid of that clutter and I can't do it.' A priest in his thirties stated the paradox for many religious: 'I'm running a million-dollar business in this school, and I have to make use of expensive gadgets in my job, yet I hope I will have the freedom to walk away from it all without undue pain when I'm asked to do so.'

Most priests saw this freedom of spirit and an ability to adapt to situations as an important aspect of their vow of poverty. A priest in his sixties spoke for three-quarters of the priests: 'What I am seeking in this vow is freedom, an independence from things.' One priest in his mid-fifties looked beyond the traditional view on vows:

The vows don't mean much to me as far as religious life is concerned. It cools my enthusiasm to get tied up in technicalities of vows. I know they are supposed to be the basis and criteria of religious life, but it is not the vows that define my way of life. My vocation does. It's the whole attitude and approach to life that we take to the various jobs we do that makes us distinctive rather than our vows.

Another priest also extended the traditional view on the vow of poverty. While realising that the vow of poverty applies to individual religious, not to the congregation as a body, he pointed out how lack of money disadvantages the poor, even in spiritual matters, and suggested how congregations could help to redress this injustice:

> The average per capita income actually determines access to the sacraments even here in Australia. You only have to compare suburbs like Woollahra with those in the west of Sydney. With the right use of material goods, religious can move against and correct this trend. They can use money coming from wealthier areas to support members of their congregation working where there is no possible income for them. This is how the vow of poverty should operate within a congregation.

He acknowledged that some congregations are already operating on this principle, but urges it should be done on a much wider scale. He firmly asserted that any interpretation of the vow of poverty as a personal use of material goods was unsophisticated and out-of-date:

> The question of rich and poor must come into the understanding of the vow of poverty and justice is an essential part of it. Poverty is related to what money can buy, that is, higher education and good health. Religious should be sensitive to the wider social, not just personal use of material goods and be prepared to protest and to clarify issues on behalf of those who cannot do it for themselves.

A growing number of religious are becoming sensitive to society's sometimes unjust use and distribution of material goods. They are not yet known for a public stand on such issues.

Personal allowances

Sisters

Because congregations, male and female, receive very few, if any, novices, have ageing members no longer earning stipends but receiving social services, and support financially some members who work in poor areas without remuneration, they are experiencing a decline in income. The smaller the congregation, the quicker the decline. There is no longer, as a forty-year-old sister remarked, 'a limitless, bottomless coffer of money to be used'. A sister in her thirties recently saw the financial state of her congregation, and her reaction was one of shock: 'I was suddenly made aware how quickly we would soon have nothing.' It brought into sharp focus for her the question 'of needing to harbour our resources for the aged, so they would be adequately cared for, yet at the same time trying to use our money productively for people in need.' Material poverty in fact may well be forced on congregations, as both a sister and brother commented. In recent years, therefore, the finances of most congregations, male and female, have been centralised, so that funds may be more profitably handled. The method of centralisation varies in detail among congregations and within any particular congregation. Basically, the central finance body of a congregation determines the percentage of income local communities contribute to it, and not all communities within any one congregation necessarily contribute the same amount: this usually depends on the income and expenditure of each community.

In some congregations the local community submits its yearly budget and this, sometimes queried and with lower estimates required, is accepted by the central finance body. Religious men and women report that for smaller communities the percentage taken from their income does sometimes cause certain hardship. A thirty-nine-year-old sister lives in such a community and is glad to experience some poverty in fact, although at one stage she said: 'I was borrowing from my personal allowance to put it into an empty community purse for groceries. It was crazy.' Money thus centralised is used for care of the elderly and ill, education and formation of members, support of members working without financial remuneration as well as those engaged in internal administration.

In some congregations the amount of the personal allowance for individual religious is determined by the major superior, in others by the local superior or by the individual in consultation with the superior. In rare cases the local community determines the personal allowance. The most frequently mentioned amount for a sister's allowance in 1986 was $60 a month but a few were managing on $45 and others were receiving $80 a month. This allowance usually covered all expenses except food, medical, dental, holiday, retreat and major travel expenses. Every sister on a personal allowance, with the exception of one, said that if some expensive item, for example a winter coat, was needed, and she did not have sufficient money, she would be expected to mention this to the superior or, in some cases, to the community in order to be subsidised. In other words, the amount is flexible, but most sisters keep within it. Not all sisters receive a personal allowance. Sometimes it is their choice to do so; sometimes the congregation or community as a whole makes the decision for all members. Sisters not receiving personal allowances ask their superior for money as their needs arise. Four sisters mentioned that they kept, without permission, money their families gave them on a fairly regular basis. One sister in her forties said a number in her congregation had what they called their 'unofficial' purse, simply because they had insufficient money for their needs.

School principals and convent bursars have access to certain monies for which accountability is not strictly enforced, and some sisters filling these roles feel they can make personal use of such monies. Sisters in a community are aware that this is sometimes done and not questioned, and they feel a certain resentment that one or two sisters in a community have direct and easy access to money for which they do not account, and so are not in the position of having to request money above what is normally given. As a fifty-one-year-old sister remarked: 'Our bursar and school principal are able to take their friends out for meals, where I just haven't the money to do so and would never ask for it. But they are able to play Lady Bountiful.' It would seem that major superiors need to re-examine the area of finance where it affects the individual religious.

The personal allowance, according to a seventy-eight-year-old sister, has helped sisters become more aware of the cost of goods and gives a choice to sisters of how to spend their money: she herself chooses to give $20 a month to charity. One forty-four-year-old sister indulges herself by collecting stamps, but forgoes photography: 'I can afford only one bad habit.' Most sisters use their money without anxiety, but some older ones have problems. A sister in her sixties often worries how she should use money: should she give her little extra to charity or use it to enjoy a film occasionally? As a sister in her seventies remarked: 'We were more secure before the changes; we knew exactly what we should do.' Responsibility and accountability in the area of personal poverty is now the individual's, not the superior's.

Brothers

Sisters appeared to be more interested than brothers and priests in money for personal use and in the methods of obtaining it: it was more of an issue for them. Male religious were far more casual in their discussion of money. One possible reason for this may be that, judging from this study, sisters as a group do not have access to as much money as male religious. Four brothers have personal allowances varying between $80 and $120 a month. The brother receiving $80 has made his personal decision to keep strictly within that amount for all his needs, while the others in his community require extra money for travel and holiday expenses. Communities of two brothers operate on an honour system: they take what they require for incidentals from a petty cash tin and ask for such items as clothes. One finds this 'always a bit of a thorn in my side': he feels embarrassed as he is the only one in the community who extracts money for sports, $7 weekly for his golf. Seven brothers ask the superior for more or less the exact money as a specific need arises, while the majority, ten brothers, obtain stipulated amounts varying from $20 to $50 as their previous amount for incidentals runs out. A brother who is a principal commented ironically: 'It's funny having to ask for $20 when, as principal of eight hundred kids, I handle hundreds of thousands of dollars.' Two brothers receive $80 and $100 respectively each month for incidentals and request extra for clothing, etc.

Priests

The same variety is apparent within congregations of priests. Seven priests ask for money as they require it; eight have access to a petty cash tin and account in a book for what they take. One priest receives $80 a month for incidentals and requests money for clothes, etc., while seven receive between $20 and $40 a month for the same incidentals. One priest has an allowance of $90, another of $80 a month which covers all his requirements except for medicine, travel and holiday expenses.

Obedience

Sisters

Religious men and women were once very sure what the vow of obedience demanded from them. They simply had to obey, quite literally, the words of superiors, because the superiors, through virtue of their position of authority, revealed the will of God to them. They conformed, sometimes with aching or angry hearts, to the law of the constitutions and to the superior because they earned salvation by being obedient. A guarantee was given. Even beyond 1960 religious men and women were familiar with the dictum: 'Keep the Rule and the Rule will keep you.' Unless their conscience clearly showed them it was a matter of sin—the only part their conscience actually played in the area of obedience—they either obeyed or, in their own eyes and in those of others, were disobedient; that is, religious who had rejected the will of God for themselves. A contemplative sister spoke about her vow of obedience:

> I never realised before I entered what it was to give up my will completely, even my judgement and ideas. Often my automatic, inward response to the superior's request is one of rejection, but then I say to myself: 'That is what Our Lord is saying to me through her, and so I am going to try to obey no matter what I feel or think.'

Few active sisters in this study are still thinking and acting in this way. But it is in recent years that some major superiors were posting lists of those being transferred from one to another community. These lists would be placed on notice boards and that would be the first the sister being transferred would know about it. An eighty-year-old sister recalled how difficult she found this, but 'I just took it. God spoke through my superior.' One sister in her early forties was told on a Wednesday that she was being transferred to an island mission in the Pacific Ocean and that she was to leave on the following Monday: there was no time for her to farewell her family, as they lived at a long distance from her.

According to most sisters, the vow of obedience as interpreted in the first half of the twentieth century had not really affected them. They had been trained to see the will of God in the superior's word and were usually prepared and happy to obey. There were two areas in which some sisters experienced difficulty in varying degrees: one, when they were transferred to a place that placed heavier demands on them; two, when they were asked to undertake work for which they felt unfitted. No mention was made of difficulty in daily life. For those sisters who did experience great trauma in obedience, the effects could be far-reaching. A sister in her thirties believes that the effects of blind obedience on some sisters have been disastrous to them as human beings:

> I have come across quite a few. They have become almost non-people. They have no identity. They hurt and they are angry about incidents ten, even twenty, years ago, when decisions were made for them. And that's true. Superiors really didn't listen then.

Today, sisters are still working through changes in the meaning of this vow. For a thirty-eight-year-old sister, 'Obedience is now bigger than something you might be asked to do by the superior. It is a commitment to a way of life.' As a thirty-year-old sister said: 'I do not see obedience as doing what I'm told; I see it as following Gospel values.' A sixty-three-year-old sister commented:

> We have moved from a very highly centralised understanding of obedience to one where we recognise God speaks through each one of us. We, as a local community, are trying to move together into a real discernment of important issues in our lives. Sometimes, depending on what the situation is, the community presents the results of their discernment to the provincial team for their discernment before any decision is reached.

A forty-two-year-old sister remarked:

There is the recognition that the Spirit works in lots of ways. If someone feels moved to a certain ministry, the superiors are open to the suggestion and so too are the community members. We are not marvellous at it, but we are trying to listen to one another.

A thirty-six-year-old sister believes that, for her,

The vow of obedience is first a listening to what is going on inside me, then a listening to the needs of my community. For example, if I want to begin some studies, I have to look at how this may affect my ministry, then at how my withdrawal from the community in order to study will affect it as a group. Finally, I have to see how what I want to study fits in with what my major superiors are planning.

Other sisters use the word 'listening' in connection with the vow of obedience, and they emphasise that time is an important factor in decision-making: it takes time to listen and to discern with people. Those in authority have a special responsibility to listen carefully.

Through her struggle with her vow of obedience, a thirty-one-year-old sister came to a greater appreciation of what religious life and obedience mean for her:

I wanted very much to live and work in a third world country, not just to be poor in a rich country. My sisters told me that I was needed in Australia. For a long time I struggled to change their opinion until, one day, I said to myself: 'What would I feel and do if they told me I could go wherever I wanted?' It was then I realised I did not want to run the affair. Someone also said to me: 'If you really feel called to live in a third world country, you don't have to stay with this congregation. You can just go.' And I knew that was true. So I realised that I had other values besides that one: it was a time for me to sort out my values. My obedience to the congregation was my first priority: I wanted that more than living in a third world country. The problem with obedience was me, not anyone else. The community waited for me to realise that; they just kept quietly saying 'No'. I felt strongly that they were at one in their decision. When occasionally someone said, 'Maybe we should agree with her', I found an interior dissenting voice saying 'No'. I realised that going where I wanted to go was not as important as doing the will of God.

A thirty-seven-year-old sister had this to say about the vow of obedience:

As I am trying to live it now, it gives me a greater sense of responsibility. I know there is a shift in power as a result, and I am trying to be sensitive to the person in authority who could feel a little more responsible than she needs to. It is an ideal to expect that people in authority will allow things to happen, so I have to accept that, at times, their own fears and doubts will be blocks, just as mine can be. And, if religious life is there for the life of the church, I think we need to be clear about obedience, which to me is about unity and discovering the author of who I am. Something of that has to be communicated to the laity, because they are struggling with that same issue at the moment. They are also coming to a new identity of themselves in church and taking more responsibility for their Christian life. Religious and laity can share a lot in this area.

Every sister was definite in her assertion that once she has put her case clearly before the superior, she would do what was asked. After mutual discernment the superior has the final word. Even though at first glance it may seem that this attitude is the same as that of the contemplative sister mentioned earlier, in principle it is very different. Ideally, both sister and superior now recognise in each other a responsible person who has facts and feelings that need to be listened to before a final decision can be made. The superior, in effect, makes her decision in partnership with the sister. She can no longer make an arbitrary decision and expect it to be obeyed in the name of the vow.

If, after consulting fully with her, the superior made a decision with which she disagreed, a sister in her forties outlined what she would do:

I would try to be as positive as possible about the situation, but if it isn't working out well after a reasonable length of time, I would go back to the superior so that we could both re-look at the situation. I would feel comfortable about that. I believe Jesus expects us to be in life-giving situations.

A fifty-eight-year-old sister had the same opinion:

> I accept the superior's word as the last one. But, in justice, I have
> always made clear to her my limitations in the particular work
> she has asked me to do. If I'm hopeless in the situation, I'd go
> back to her and I am confident she would listen to me.

Not all sisters experience this confidence in superiors. A
sister in her late forties explained that she was unhappy
about a recent transfer, because, although she had represented
her case, she believed that a decision was taken in the first
place without sufficient information and was then upheld.
She obeyed, but the lack of what she saw as consultation still
rankles. Another sister in her early forties does not think that
superiors in her congregation really consult sisters about
their transfers. For them, she said, consultation means that
'the superior tells the individual face to face what is going to
happen instead of informing her by letter. There is no true
listening or mutual decision-making.'

Some sisters now see the superior as one who may be
called in as an objective third party. When a fifty-seven-year-
old sister and her school principal interpreted a principle
from different viewpoints, there was a resulting deadlock.
The former felt so strongly about the issue she was prepared
to disobey the principal. Both were happy to ask the superior
to discuss the issue with them and 'she helped me to see the
position for the principal as well as for myself. The situation,
with her help, was resolved amicably.' More than one sister
sees the superior as one who enables, encourages and
challenges the community. Obedience now means being
positively active in one's life.

It was not always so for a thirty-seven-year-old sister:

> At times I used to expect those in authority to work out what was
> happening inside me and what I really wanted. Which was
> childish, because if I didn't know, how could they understand?
> I'm not so negative about superiors now. I can accept that they,
> too, are often unsure and struggling to know what is the best
> thing to do.

A forty-year-old sister is pondering her future:

I am wondering whether I want to continue teaching for the next twenty years or so or if there is another way I can more positively work for the church. I have to take responsibility in this: it is not the responsibility of superiors to come to me about a change in ministry.

A sister in her late forties admitted she had been seriously thinking about her vow of obedience in the previous twelve months. Happy in her community and successful in her ministry, she has asked herself:

Have I the inner freedom to move if I were asked? The movement in obedience has been from the superior requiring me to do things, to me checking out my inner freedom. I gave obedience and allegiance in matters affecting my life to a major superior whom I greatly admired. Now I ask myself, would I give the same allegiance and obedience to a major superior whom I could not admire? Was my former obedience to the woman or to the vision? I think that, if what I was asked to do went against loyalty or my morality, I would not do it. Otherwise I would. For example, if I was asked by a tyrannical superior to make a radical change in my ministry for which I could see no valid reason, I would obey. Because I believe very much in what we're on about as a congregation, I would have an obligation to stay and maintain the vision that I believe in and to hand that vision on to others.

'Freedom to obey' was a phrase used by a few sisters. Two, for example, had each decided to ask permission to redirect their ministry. Before doing so, they reflected on whether they had the freedom to ask, that is, they did not want to ask permission until they felt they could accept a refusal in peace.

As a result of the new thinking about the vow of obedience, the one in authority today faces difficulties unknown to the superior of yesteryear. A forty-year-old sister finds her role as superior very, very difficult.

It is the difference in expectations that sisters have of me. I do not want to measure up to the role expected of me by the older sisters. I can't be a mother figure making the decisions for them. I feel badly about that, because I think they see me as heartless and unconcerned for them. I expect them to take on responsibility for themselves as well as for the group as a whole. They find that very difficult. Then there is a younger sister with a different set of values: there's almost a collision of values and she gets frustrated by some attitudes of the older ones. At times I feel the meat in the sandwich.

Other superiors, including an ex-major superior, experience much the same problem. They feel caught in a situation in which they cannot move freely. As one superior in her fifties said:

> I am not sure whether God is asking me to operate according to the present interpretation of the role of superior, which is held by the majority of the sisters. Or whether he expects me, as a person, to be critically assessing that interpretation of my role and perhaps following one I believe to be more life-giving for the sisters.

She has not yet resolved the problem, common to many in positions of authority today.

Over the years of living memory there has been no visible change in the external behaviour of the sister in regard to the vow of obedience: all interviewees were adamant that they would finally accept the superior's decision. Now, however, the process towards that decision varies. Rarely does the superior give a command without first talking about it and listening to the one concerned. Occasionally lip-service is given to the principle of consultation. In the majority of cases, sisters are struggling to implement what that principle implies. Obedience is seen as a genuine listening to the needs of the individual concerned, the local community and the congregation before those responsible make the decision. Even though the individual allows that in case of differing opinions the superior has the final word, she sees the decision as mutual. Obedience also means that the individual must, when appropriate, approach the superior with suggestions; for example, for a new ministry or change in lifestyle. It has been a move from blind obedience to the individual sister and superior, and often a community, making a truly informed, responsible, and above all, a mutually caring decision.

Brothers

When asked had the vow of obedience affected his life, a brother in his forties answered in amazement: 'Yes. It would be strange if it and the other vows didn't do so.' No example of effects, dramatic or otherwise, were offered. Two self-confessed independent and headstrong brothers had much the same reaction, but in their cases, clashes with authority came over school matters, clashes a lay teacher might have with a principal. Nine brothers asserted they had had no hassles with this vow, some because of their temperament, others because they had not been asked to do anything to which they objected.

The remaining brothers admitted experiencing varying degrees of difficulty with obedience, which were all connected with transfers. Transfers do not occur regularly. A brother in his seventies had changed communities seventeen times; one in his early forties, four times. The first difficulty for all brothers arose from natural repugnance to a severance from their community, their school situation and the friends they had made, but as a brother in his sixties pointed out, 'This was something that teachers in the state school system had to accept.' Knowing that they would never remain permanently in any one place, brothers were on the whole philosophical about transfers. Admitting it was usually a wrench, a brother in his thirties was very positive in his thinking:

> I've been uprooted several times. I hate being changed from a school where I'm happy and secure, know all the staff and the kids, have lots to do at weekends with my friends, but I know my new community will open up all those possibilities, too. It would be a matter again of building up more friendships and I know my horizons will be broadened. Underneath my initial resentment and frustration I'm basically happy enough about a move. It's not long before there's even a sense of excitement.

Brothers invariably objected to the method whereby transfers were once made. One brother spoke for many:

I used to think I was lost in a large machine, and I've kicked against the goad in that respect. I'd be in a place a couple of years, then I'd get a slip of paper with a transfer on it. Off I'd go, and in another two or three years there'd be another slip of paper.

Other brothers read their transfer on a list posted on their notice board. Today, as with sisters and priests, consultation takes place between a major superior and an individual before a transfer is made. They are still posted on notice boards, but the individuals concerned have already been consulted and know their new destination. Obedience, as a brother in his forties said, has become a listening process between superior and the individual and a decision is worked out in dialogue. A brother in his late fifties said his last transfer was an exception: usually consulted and offered a choice of two or three places, he was given no choice in his last transfer. 'It was a clear case of swap.' He understood the reasons behind the transfer.

Today it is extremely difficult to transfer brothers from one school to another, because of the number of lay teachers on the staff who can't be moved to accommodate an individual brother. For obvious reasons a certain brother had to come out of this school, and I was the only possible substitute. I went grudgingly, so I guess I didn't look at my vow of obedience in the correct light.

The problem of inserting religious teachers into schools is more common among brothers' congregations than among sisters', as the former have a far higher proportion of religious in schools than the latter: it may mean less real consultation in the future.

Brothers have confidence in their major superiors. The attitude of a brother in his forties is that of many others: 'I've never had to protest against a move, but if I did, I am certain my superiors would listen.' Another brother said: 'They are trying to do the best thing by me, so I should be prepared to go along with what they want, as they have the overview of the province. I can't see any point in bucking the system.'

As most brothers see the vow of obedience in connection

with transfers, they are reasonably happy with the existing situation. Two brothers, however, one in his seventies, the other in his forties, would like to see greater collegiality. The latter spelt out his opinion:

> I'm uneasy when only a few know what the hell is going on, and all the decisions are made out there away from where they're meant to be implemented. I've had to resign myself to this model, but I believe as much input from as many people as possible should be given to the group making the decision, and the group should share discernment on a faith level before making a decision.

The brother in his seventies cannot envisage many superiors being able to handle such decision-making, and also admits that in a large province such a method might be impractical. Only one brother in his early fifties wanted superiors to take more definite decisions by themselves. 'We need clear direction,' he said. 'We're drifting too easily into what we as individuals want to do.'

In day-to-day affairs the majority of brothers were not conscious of their vow of obedience. Linked with the vow, however, were courtesies most brothers acknowledged. Some, for example, believed that superiors have a right to know in general where they are and what they are doing. A young brother goes along with this principle in theory:

> One of the reasons I don't always tell him where I am going is because I go out so frequently and am often back late at night. He's an old guy, and if I tell him what's happening, he sighs, 'How can you keep this up? How's your health?' So the less he knows, the less he worries. Otherwise, it's too much of a burden for him.

Happy that he himself can now make many decisions that ten years ago could not be made without the superior's permission, a brother in his late forties still sees the superior as a guide, one with whom he wants to talk about his personal affairs. Another brother said: 'Superiors are now pretty reasonable. If you go and ask for things you think you can get and for which you've worked out a fair case, you generally find they're amenable to it.' This attitude is a far cry from an earlier period when, as a brother in his fifties remarked, 'We almost had to genuflect to the superior.'

Priests

Priests, on the other hand, had little to say on the vow of obedience. Eleven dismissed it summarily, saying it had no impact on their lives. Whatever difficulties the remainder experienced had been connected with transfers: 'Any change', as a priest in his sixties commented, 'is difficult for me, and I still kick against the goad when I'm transferred.' A priest in his late forties wryly smiled as he recalled his greatest difficulty in obedience:

After my ordination my provincial asked whether I'd like more study overseas. As I'd just finished nine years of study immediately after finishing school, I said definitely no. The next week I got a letter to say the ticket was bought, the passport coming, and I'd be beginning studies overseas in a fortnight and then he wished me good luck.

That was the old-style obedience. Today, he pointed out, he would want to know all the reasons behind an order, would want to talk through his objections, consider what he personally wanted and the good of the congregation before he assumed responsibility for this response. He concluded: 'I'd need to have very strong reasons for refusing. I did once, and my superiors listened and gracefully accepted my refusal.' A man in his sixties, however, is happy to obey today as he did twenty years ago. He explained his attitude:

After being a lifetime in one situation I was ordered off to the outback and I cried about it. An old man crying! But then I reminded myself that for years I had been telling kids to obey their parents and here I was, still bucking against obedience. So I went off to what were the best years of my life, which is one of the best things about obedience in religious life: if you do what you're told, even when you don't want to, the experience ends up as being really good.

Formerly, a thirty-four-year-old priest explained, obedience meant sacrificing your will: 'Today it means directing one's will to another. That means great insecurity, although something tells me it's also freedom.' Another man in his thirties defined obedience for himself: 'It is not so much accepting what you are told to do, but being responsible for what you are doing.' Individual responsibility was emphasised by several priests. 'Obedience', said one in his sixties, 'means "to listen" and I have to listen to my superiors. But I am the one to assess the situation and make the decision to obey or not, and I have a responsibility to make sure my response is honest.' Another priest in his sixties sees himself even more actively involved in the vow: 'I take initiatives. I don't sit back and wait for the superior to speak. I also have a responsibility to keep my superior informed about what I'm doing and why I'm doing it.' One priest in his thirties was the only one to point out that consultations are not always possible in the area of obedience. A chapter, consisting of elected representatives of members of a congregation, can make decisions affecting the direction the congregation will take and sometimes the lives of individuals. 'The hardest thing', said this priest in his thirties, 'is following a chapter decision you don't agree with. You just have to submit in obedience.'

Conclusion

With a more wholesome, realistic attitude towards the vow of chastity, religious men and women have come to appreciate the importance of friends within their lives, thus encouraging within themselves a maturity and a spirituality denied to most religious of yesteryear. It is very clear, however, no matter how great the support of their friends, religious will inevitably have problems with their vow of chastity if they do not find their communities accepting and welcoming places.

As religious assume greater responsibility for their own lives a change is seen in their attitudes towards the vow of poverty. Most religious take for granted television, videos, cars, holidays, sabbaticals in Australia and overseas, opportunities for overseas study and for spiritual renewal courses. Yet, more than ever before, they are questioning exactly what this vow means. While those who accept material poverty as the basis of their vow are worried that they are not living up to its demands, some see it as an anomaly, and others interpret it as poverty of spirit. Those most in contact with poorer sections of people see justice as an inherent component of their vow. These, a few religious sisters in this study, have chosen to align themselves with the poor and marginalised peoples. This, for them, means not only living in the neighbourhood of the poor, but also speaking out with the poor and sometimes for the poor against injustice and oppression.

The vow of poverty could be questioned only after religious discovered that the vow of obedience means more than merely assenting to the commands of superiors. Most religious hold that true obedience is possible only after they have thought for themselves, talked to superiors about what they think and how they feel and made a free, responsible decision with the superior.

A considerable number of religious, particularly sisters, no longer examine themselves on their observance of the three vows. They rarely think about them as such. Sisters, like a forty-two-year-old, are saying: 'Vows divide my life into compartments. I prefer a wholistic approach and would like one commitment, not three.' A thirty-nine-year-old sister thinks more in terms of being a disciple of Jesus and discovering her story in his: 'I find the vows somewhat artificial. They seem tacked on to give structure to my commitment to discipleship as a religious.' Religious, however, are trying to live the principles underlying the vows and place their emphasis more on a simple lifestyle adapted to the needs of those they serve.

Living in community 5

Sisters

*T*hirty years ago it was easy to describe a religious community. It was a group of religious men or women working together in the same ministry, living together under one roof, obeying the same superior, praying the same prayers together, wearing identical clothing and following the same daily pattern of living. They shared everything in common. Community life was designed to separate religious as much as possible from what was called 'the world' and fostered language and customs peculiar to religious life. There are few religious women today who would not be familiar with the programme of daily activities as outlined by a ninety-year-old sister when she spoke about community life seventy years ago.

HORARIUM: 1916

5.25 a.m.	Bell for rising.
5.45 a.m.	Morning prayers. Points for meditation read.
6.00 a.m.	Meditation.
6.30 a.m.	Morning Office.
6.45 a.m.	Mass.
7.15 a.m.	Spiritual reading.
7.50 a.m.	Breakfast.
8.15 a.m.	Departure for school.
4.30 p.m.	Recreation.
5.00 p.m.	Rosary; Litany of the Blessed Virgin; Afternoon Office.
6.00 p.m.	Spiritual reading.
6.15 p.m.	Dinner.
6.45 p.m.	Evening prayers.
7.00 p.m.	School work — preparation of lessons, correction of books; study.
8.00 p.m.	Recreation.
9.00 p.m.	Night prayers. Points for meditation read.
10.00 p.m.	Lights out.

This ninety-year-old sister elaborated further:

> We received little of the school fees, as they were needed to
> maintain the school, so we took in boarders and gave music
> lessons to make some money. This meant we took it in turns to
> supervise the boarders every moment out of school hours: we
> might miss recreation, but we always had to make up our
> prayers if we were absent at the time the community said them.
> During the weekend, we cleaned the convent and the school,
> washed clothes, gave music lessons and extra tuition to weak
> pupils, visited parents, hospitals and lonely old people. I was
> young in those days and didn't feel any pressure. There were
> chinks of time here and there for myself.

Occasionally there was a highlight to the week: a priest
would drive a few sisters to another convent for Sunday
afternoon or take them on a picnic. But the lives of the
sisters, as a sixty-four-year-old remarked, revolved around
work, the Rule and 'getting one's prayers said'.

For some, a similar community life existed until very recent
times. A sister in her thirties, for example, told of regulations
seven years ago almost identical with those mentioned by the
ninety-year-old sister:

> The day was not only totally carved up, but we had all sorts of
> rules about not ironing after 7.30 p.m., not running water before
> or after certain times. There were so many added little things one
> should or should not do.

Abiding by the rules was the name of the game. Even
at the time of this study, in 1986, a thirty-nine-year-old sister
in one congregation was wearing full religious habit, and
living a fully structured day in her community. A few
congregations still have set times for rising together, morning
and evening prayers and recreation. Within other congregations, communities of older sisters programme their day so
that they do most things in common.

Sisters were adamant that the atmosphere within the
convent of yesteryear depended largely on the type of woman
the superior was. Responsible for the community's spiritual
and physical welfare, she was held in reverential awe, and, as

a seventy-eight-year-old sister commented, her wishes were carried out as being the will of God. In some congregations, it was always the superior who initiated conversation at recreation; in others, the senior sisters shared the privilege. Seniority, therefore, played an important part in community life. A sister in her mid-thirties said:

As a young sister I found I was being watched, assessed, evaluated and corrected if I put a foot wrong. You had to appease some by going along with what they wanted. I suffered a lot from their vigilance, but I suppressed my reactions out of a need to belong, to be accepted by the community. Some of the older sisters did give me support, and I knew they cared for me.

When she joined her first community fourteen years ago, a forty-year-old sister was dismayed at the expectations placed upon her by the community: 'Sisters wanted to put a stamp on you, so you would be like every one else. If you were gifted in any way, there was a suspicion of that gift.' The community's watchfulness ensured conformity. A sister in her mid-forties recalled: 'If a sister even forgot to wear her rosary beads externally, it was suspected she had deliberately decided to step out of line.'

Reactions to this earlier pattern of community life varied from the forty-seven-year-old sister who spontaneously spoke of it as 'bloody awful' to the sixty-three-year-old who, an organised person herself, found early community life much easier than the pattern of the present day. The common life was community life, and because doing the same things together gave sisters a feeling of unity, some, like a fifty-year-old, still prefer the earlier style: 'There were sisters with spirit and life. Our community life was far from dull.' A forty-eight-year-old sister said: 'On the whole, there was more happiness in those days than there is today. We had more community life because we had more time together at recreation. We took more interest in each other.'

A fifty-nine-year-old sister commented: 'The structures at least made sure that everyone was absorbed in what was happening.' Few sisters referred to the external sign of unity, the religious habit, symbol of structures and denial of femininity. Those who mentioned it did so because of the sufferings they had endured in the heat of inland towns. A fifty-seven-year-old sister said:

> It could be one hundred and nineteen degrees for days on end. We wore pleated black serge habits with thick petticoats and, on our heads, lighter serge dominos and veils over white starched coifs and forehead bands. Our guimps, often made out of celluloid, covered our chests. I don't know how we survived.

Community life, however, can no longer be equated with a common ministry, dress and lifestyle. Different attitudes stemming from Vatican II and changing values in Australian culture, together with the move from institutional to individual ministry, have largely swept away the rules minutely regulating the hours and behaviour of the sisters. Structures today have flexibility and are made by the local community as a group. The community, usually with at least one new member, meet at the beginning of the year, sometimes for two days, to discuss their hopes and ideals, to plan objectives for the year ahead and to decide when and how they will meet as a group. The new structures encourage sisters to express their own views and to listen to those of others. Weekly structures, other than daily gatherings for meals and, sometimes, prayers, are the norm — and in some communities even these are not structured. 'They are there as a help to an end, not as a controlling mechanism,' explained a seventy-one-year-old sister. The less structured set-up reflects an understanding of religious life based not on rules but on relationship of each with the Lord and with each other.

A thirty-eight-year-old sister lives in a community of ten who set aside one night a week for themselves: they meet for a leisurely dinner at 6 p.m., pray together informally, then remain talking with one another until 9 or 10 o'clock. A thirty-five-year-old sister lives with five sisters. Her community meet each Monday night for twice-monthly business meetings and for a twice-monthly review of their community life during the previous fortnight. Once a month the community have a special time; they meet for prayer at 5.30 p.m., and dine together before talking or watching a video for the rest of the evening. Each Tuesday morning they meet for a short time to discuss their constitutions and share their reflections on them. The variety of such arrangements even within one congregation is wide: few central governing councils now legislate the structures for local communities. Personal prayer is the responsibility of the individual. One sister in her early thirties, for example, chooses to rise at 5.15 a.m. in order to have time for yoga exercises as a direct preparation for her hour of prayer. 'I have to have private prayer,' she claimed, 'or I'm a wipe-out.' Sisters frequently expressed their appreciation for personal prayer. A forty-year-old sister said: 'We are now praying, where before we used to say set prayers.'

Time for informal relationships, usually on a weekly basis, is sometimes slotted into the community pattern. As a thirty-seven-year-old sister explained:

We have to become more conscious that we are people who, despite appearances and differences, share the same basic desires, yearnings and longings. Our life-thrust is the same, and the only way we can recognise and be supported by that is really talking to one another, giving one another time.

A sister in her mid-thirties expressed the need to meet on more than a superficial level: 'We have to take time with things that are really crucial to our being able to live the religious life.' When this happens, sisters change. A fifty-three-year-old sister said:

I consider I lost my humanity thirty-three years ago, and in the last four years I have rediscovered it through the relationship we have built up in this community of six. You have to cultivate the art of living together for this to happen.

Of those who gave their opinion of an ideal size for a community, two-thirds preferred between five and seven sisters. According to sisters favouring this size of community, its advantages reflect their hopes and create opportunities for their reality. A community between five and seven sisters is small enough for members to relate with one another, to talk together in depth about their ideals and hopes, to arrange flexible structures for meals and prayers, to form one group

92

without sub-groups emerging, to share fully in group functions and responsibilities and to allow privacy for the individual. It is large enough to allow some sisters to be absent without leaving one or two by themselves, to absorb one incompatible or psychologically damaged sister without unduly affecting the life of the community and to enjoy a balance of ages and experiences.

The basis of community life is in the process of changing. A forty-eight-year-old sister believed that the major change in community life

is that the emphasis on the external has been reduced and the challenge has been to internalise values. The freedom is there for sisters to live life with very varied values within the one system. The possibility is there for sisters to confront directly their own humanity. Religious life is allowing sisters to discover themselves as women rather than staying in a cocoon of goodness. No longer is there one model of what we're on about as a religious congregation, and yet there is something in our vision uniting us. At the most fundamental level we are united, but at the peripheral there's incredible variation both in terms of external ways of being and internal ways of relating and being.

This 'incredible variation both in terms of external ways of being and internal ways of relating and being' lies at the heart of the important issue of community with which sisters are grappling. As individuals, many have come to experience new attitudes and values and have at last gained a feeling of being themselves and appreciated, but they realise that the community as such has not achieved similar growth. A forty-three-year-old sister expressed her confusion:

We have changed habits. We have broken down structures at community level. We have people moving into different ministries. We have offered sisters changes in their spiritual development . . . but I don't experience a new form of religious life. Some think that ministry will create a new form, but I'm not too sure about that. In my congregation I see us contracting to fewer convents, remaining irrelevant in our lifestyle. We used to be relevant to people thirty years ago. Not now. We have to show them something in our lives that makes sense and meaning to them. I'm not sure what that something is.

As a thirty-nine-year-old sister said: 'As a group our ideas have gone forward, but not our practices. We haven't integrated changes in our thinking with changes that need to take place in our behaviour.'

A number of sisters under fifty years agree with a forty-two-year-old:

Existing changes have been cosmetic, a matter of rearranging externals without altering the essence of religious life. We have adaptation, not genuine renewal. And the large group are content to work within the existing situation.

And a sister in her mid-forties pointed out: 'We are still reacting to the restrictions of the past. We are in a transitional period: we know what we're not about, but we are not sure what we are about.' A seventy-three-year-old sister commented on what she believes is a tendency of sisters to over-emphasise their community concerns: 'There is too much talk about how the congregation is going — will it survive? What will happen to us in our old age? We should be more interested in our ministry than in our own survival.'

According to a forty-one-year-old sister, the very freedom individual sisters now possess proves an obstacle in the way of a fundamental community change:

Some are happy with the situation as it is. So, even though a lot of us see that community life needs to be different, we are held back by our feeling of responsibility for the ones who don't want to make any more changes. Do we divide the sisters into two styles of communities, or do we struggle to form community with sisters holding different values?

In the latter case, sisters approximately between fifty and sixty-five years of age experience pressure as the buffer group between the older ones, who are largely content with existing community changes, and the younger ones, who are calling for more basic changes in attitude. Some, wanting to avoid any appearance of division, agree with a thirty-one-year-old sister:

Changes can be made the god. If it is the Spirit moving, we will not crush people. If a sister is unwilling to accept change, we have to ask how we can accept and nurture her at this stage. We have to provide a climate in community in which all can live and move at their own pace.

The tension of living in a group of sisters with different visions of community life prompts some sisters to consider living alone. Their appreciation of the importance of community in religious life prevents most from taking this step. A forty-eight-year-old sister has contemplated this solution:

> I certainly sigh for the flesh-pot of a flat, but I know very well that, if I took it, it would be the end of me in some ways. I need the bonding of a community, a shared vision. Community for me, ultimately, is bigger than the local one. It is these people with whom I share an identity, very much a congregational sense of community.

Others are facing the same question. The situation becomes more difficult when, in a community, the majority are at least twenty years older than the youngest. This is the case for a forty-one-year-old sister who feels keenly the pressure of the expectations of the four older sisters in her community. She said: 'I am questioning whether community living is possible for me or whether it is militating against my ministry too much. They do not understand my values or the pressures in my work.'

Sometimes the minority are trying to support themselves on an inter-community level. Some sisters in different communities of the one congregation have formed self-chosen groups of four or five who meet regularly once a week for prayer and review of the previous week. They have the same ideals and receive support from each other. The scheme is possible only in a city. One member of such a group, who is fifty-five years old, realises that such groups may create a division within their congregation, but 'unless we do something, we shall just die out'.

The very emphasis on and confusion about what is community indicates that therein may lie the key to the future of religious life. Although coming from a minority, one trend is clear: a number of sisters wish to insert themselves into ordinary life and to be seen to do so. One forty-year-old sister reflected:

Religious used to see themselves as very much in another world, and they had distorted views of life, of work and of sex. Humanity was negated. The world was a sinful place, and the big thing was to save your soul and get to heaven. Whereas now we see God is here with us, and so we are emphasising life and accepting our humanity. It is important to live the same kind of life as everyone else in the street and to be seen as trying to live the Gospel values in that ordinary life.

Another sister in her forties said:

We should be seen as ordinary women, because that's who we are, but I would hope that people would look at us and say: 'They lead ordinary lives, but there is something different about them. What is their vision of life that makes the difference?' Our communities will have to be deeply immersed in Gospel values for that question to be asked. I don't see us living that way at the moment.

Sisters thinking along these lines have now become aware of a new dimension to community: they believe that as a unit the community should have a special ministry of its own to people today. This is what four sisters, living in what many would see as an ideal community, have realised. One of its members, thirty-six years old, described their present arrangement and possible future development:

We do not use the Prayer of the Church. As an active congregation we don't see it suits our lifestyle. We pray from life. We stop and look at what has happened to us in the previous twenty-four hours and pray out of that. Each sister has her own ministry, and we have great mobility and social contact with people. We have no oppressive structures, and we challenge one another in our commitment and ministry. Our community is very supportive and caring. We are finding, however, that it is too supportive, too comfortable and it is still on a complex of church, school, presbytery and convent. We have no neighbours as such. We don't feel part of the local scene, nor do we contribute to it. This is our present challenge. We find it is our work in schools that is keeping us from local involvement. We envisage moving to a place where what comes first is our community lifestyle, which would involve us with the local people and their concerns. We could then see what work we could do.

Together with a small group of sisters living in a small country town, a thirty-five-year-old sister is working along these same principles:

People used to believe that sisters living separate, isolated lives were the holy ones. We were saints they could revere, not imitate. That's changed. The thing that is so exciting for me, other than the way we live together, is that sense of how we are for the people of the area. There is a sense that it is just not me — it is who we are as religious women for this group of people in the town. People need to feel that we accept them in their daily life; we do not judge them if they don't come to church. We share a common humanity. We do disappoint a few because we are so darned ordinary — the mystery has gone.

The very ordinariness of our lives today and the visibility of our relationship with each other encourages people to find meaning and God in their lives, which are so like ours. I sense we are touching people's lives at a totally different level than even ten years ago. That is what our religious community is about: inserting itself into the neighbourhood community.

Such an insertion will have repercussions not only on community life but also on religious life in general.

Brothers

The brothers interviewed saw their ministry more closely tied with their community life than did sisters. When, for example, brothers were asked to say something about their first experience of community life, sixteen out of twenty-two (three from clerical congregations were first engaged in domestic work) included some aspect of ministry in their immediate reply. Typical opening remarks came from a brother in his mid-thirties: 'I first went to a welcoming, supportive community. I felt very privileged to have been sent to one of our biggest schools and it was a great thrill to have my own class at last.' His remarks highlight another feature common to brothers: they have a keen sense of being sent to a community to do a job and they have an awareness of a career structure within their system. One possible factor governing the brothers' attitude was their congregations' emphasis on professional training for the ministry. All or part of their training began immediately after they left the novitiate. Brothers had a more normal professional development than did many sisters, thus coming into contact with their lay peers, which usually resulted in a mature option for religious life at the end of training. As a brother in his forties said:

The relatively free-wheeling lifestyle of university contrasted vividly with a high degree of seemingly unnecessary regimentation in the monastery, and so, during my studies, I was forced to re-look at my vocation before coming to a conscious decision to remain.

Twenty years ago, then, the average brother was arriving at his first community well prepared for his work and often commencing further studies that provided him with extra pressure but also with an interest that took him beyond the community and the classroom. For him, as for the sister, structures minutely detailing divisions within the day and order of seniority were rigidly observed. The superiors were, in the words of a brother in his fifties, 'the power brokers. They were in their places for six years, then often swapped. It was common for a man to do this for thirty years.'

Although it was seen as necessary 'to keep in with the boss', as he had such power in the community, some brothers set out, as one put it, 'to beat the system', and in that they found a form of bonding. One or two felt loneliness in community, but several young brothers clubbed together as a group and managed to circumvent minor, irritating regulations. 'Twenty years ago,' said a brother, 'I wasn't supposed to read the newspapers, but,' smiling happily, 'I managed to get to them.'

Brothers in clerical congregations found life more difficult. Completely segregated from the priests, they were yet able to see and suffer from discriminations: for example, they were not allowed to use cars and were often expected to caretake schools while priests were on holidays. The majority of brothers claimed to have seen community life as a challenge, and as one remarked, 'a good experience learning to live with men of different ages and opinions'. Sports, high on the agenda, helped brothers cope with their initiation into community life. A brother in his forties recalled how when he and his peers were in their mid-twenties, brothers ten or so years older would pull them into various sporting activities during the weekend. Football matches between city communities were often arranged.

The following changes in the life of brothers came during the late 1960s and 1970s. The first three are recognised as the most important, but the others are not in order of priority.

- The values and needs of the individual are recognised.
- Far more is left to the initiative and responsibility of the individual brother.
- There is a desire for more open and honest communication.
- Friendship with women is more acceptable.
- Monasteries are seen more as homes; parents are now permitted to stay with brothers.
- Brothers feel more comfortable approaching major superiors to offer ideas or to make requests, so there is a sense of active involvement in the administration of the congregation.
- The superior is in an advisory and leadership capacity and does not pretend to have all the answers.
- The community now plans its own structures.
- Lay brothers have been absorbed into the external ministry. Of those interviewed, one is a superior, another a deputy principal, the third is a counsellor within a school.
- Some brothers are moving out of traditional ministries.

The majority of brothers are happy with their present community lifestyle. Any change they foresee is one of degree, not of kind. Difficulties they may experience come from individual brothers unwilling to adapt to change in structures and form of prayer, not from the community format envisaged by the congregation as a whole. They know what they require from community and most agree with the definition offered by a brother in his mid-forties: 'For me, community means relating to brothers whenever there is a wish or need to do so. Community is family to me. It is where I share my experiences and feel accepted.' A seventy-one-year-old brother, however, rejects the image of family for a community: 'You can develop as a person in community provided you assume adult responsibility and refuse to allow yourself to be looked after by the community.'

Although appreciating their greater freedom, about a quarter of the brothers are concerned that there is at present an undue emphasis on the freedom of the individual and little, if any, on the individual's responsibility to the congregation and to his community in particular. A brother in his forties said:

We are beginning to suffer the legacy of an understandable but exaggerated reaction against community life of former times. From a lifestyle that fostered somewhat infantile dependence among community members, some of us are swinging to unmitigated independence, which plays havoc with community life. I see myself as fortunate in being with a group who takes that seriously, and we often talk about the ideal of inter-dependence.

Some brothers are concerned lest prayers by jettisoned. One in his early fifties said: 'Some communities don't have Mass daily. Brothers just say they go to Mass when they feel like it.' Another in his seventies was of like mind: brothers, he said, tend to cut down on prayers. Brothers also cope with an ageing community. One in his fifties explained some effects of this on community life:

Younger men can't find people their own age in community now, so they feel the need to look elsewhere for companionship. We can't blame them, but it breaks down the community, especially in holiday time. As they are also under pressure to become more and more qualified, they have to be absent sometimes from community exercises such as prayer and recreation. The older men miss their enthusiasm and energy. Things are quieter without them.

A brother in his forties has seen another effect. When there is a very small number of young brothers in community, the older ones, if they wish, have the power to block any change they do not want. The result, he said, is polarisation, with the young brothers becoming as intolerant as the older and seeking their support and friends outside the community. The smaller community in the country areas has sometimes found a solution to its size and isolation. In one case, religious men and women meet regularly six times a year on an inter-congregational basis: 'We have come to believe', said a brother in his forties, 'that we are all in this together, and we need each other. It is a significant change to have this wider community of men and women.'

Priests

Structures regulating times for rising, meals, etc., once dominated community life for religious priests as they did for brothers and sisters. There had been the expectation, as several priests pointed out, that the community should and would supply all the support the members needed, and that the members would participate in everything together. According to a priest in his late thirties:

> The old community model was right wing, with every emotion repressed under the religious habit, so that conformity was the ideal in order to present to people a high profile of unity and public witness to religious values.

'We shared a common vision,' said a priest in his forties, 'and were very uniform in the way we shared that.' As one priest remarked: 'The question was "Could you conform?" rather than "Could you think for yourself?"' A sixty-two-year-old priest commented:

> In a sense it was too spiritual; there was little consideration of our humanity. There were laws that a lot of us didn't obey, yet the laws were still there and had their influence. A strained type of life . . .

The superior was often a benevolent dictator and felt he was responsible for whatever the community did, good or bad.

Only a few priests expressed a different concept of community life from that of sisters and brothers. One in his sixties said:

> Community does not equal religious men living together. Basically, obedience constitutes your belonging to community. Because you are sent on mission by your congregation, you are in community whether you live alone or among one hundred members of your congregation. This is very different from saying a group of religious form a community in a particular house.

For those supporting this concept, ministry is paramount. Because he holds this concept, a priest in his sixties disapproves of a trend he sees among religious women.

> I'm opposed to groups of four or six religious living for the sake of community in small houses, because I don't think it is productive for the ministry in the long run, and it leaves religious off the hook a great deal. Sooner or later they've got to face up to an institutional life and, if you can't live under a bureaucracy, you can't live in modern society.

He added: 'As far as I am concerned as an active religious, even spiritual well-being is a means to the end of ministry just as good health is a means to an end and not an end in itself.'

Two priests recognised the primacy of community. One in his late fifties stated that, by directing a re-examination of their founder's charism and directives, Vatican II altered his congregation's emphasis from that on ministry to community: 'Community for us now means witnessing to the Gospel principles stressed in our Rules. Without community we don't exist.' A priest in a contemplative congregation agreed:

> From the 1960s we placed more importance on the monastic vocation, and there is evidence that men are joining us for this and not for the priesthood. We are returning to the original monasticism, where the aim is personal holiness.

It appears that religious priests are not as affected as are sisters by their earlier community life. One priest in his forties gave an explanation of this:

> The very ministry of priests takes them out of their communities and gives them another area of interest and support that sisters and brothers didn't always have. Hence some priests had an opportunity for another community formed by lay people among whom they worked. This made it easier for them to drop the values and customs of large religious communities.

Together with other religious, priests appreciated the greater freedom and trust given to the individual in community after Vatican II. Where authority previously controlled religious people, today it helps them achieve their potential. A priest in his forties said:

> Those in administration are trying very hard to see how God wants to work within the lives of each member. They are making people realise they are precious and important. We are all now coming to realise that, although we have a common vision, individuals express it differently.

A priest in his mid-fifties remarked: 'The most wonderful thing in religious life today is that you can be yourself, and this adds to the richness of everyone's lives and to the image we present to people.' Individuals have to assume responsibility for their own lives and the degree to which this is encouraged varies with the congregation. A priest in his mid-thirties remarked:

> The intention is now to respect men's maturity and individuality. That has sometimes resulted in instability and uncertainty, but it made me, for the first time, really face up to the most basic thing in my life—prayer—and where it came in my life.

According to a priest in his fifties, power struggles once common in communities are now lessening, and religious priests have a greater sense of participating in both community and congregational decisions. Rules have become guidelines for many: 'I no longer live by a Rule because the Rule orders this and that. I live it now', said one priest in his late fifties, 'because I want to be here and I make my own choice to obey.' A priest in his sixties said: 'Vision and values are now acknowledged as being more important than the slavish interpretation of rules.' A priest in his seventies expressed his excitement at the changes:

> The community has become more open, realistic and helpful to people. We are more concerned with the quality of living in community and we no longer withdraw to our own world. Religious really should be ordinary Christian-living people following the Christian message fully in order to assist others to do so.

There are priests who prefer the more traditional community, and there is resulting tension when others in the same community do not. A superior in his mid-thirties is caught in this tension of holding 'the old and the new' together: 'My main worry is trying to co-ordinate and keep on a reasonably even keel a group ranging from thirty years to eighty-five who are wanting to go a hundred different ways.' He said he often feels angry about the responsibility he is asked to carry and the exterior attitudes he believes his role imposes upon him. To respect the needs of younger men and the wishes of the more traditional men, one priest suggested that religious of like mind should form communities. Others would see this as unwisely divisive.

One congregation is re-assessing recent changes, and a priest in his twenties spoke about the results of this re-assessment:

> Silence has been re-introduced at certain times and in certain places. We have definite times for rising, praying, eating and recreating together. There is now more emphasis on wearing the religious habit. The younger priests really pushed for these things, and I'm pleased with them. I find regularity a great help because everyone is with me.

What this young priest said was echoed, but not supported or approved, by a priest in his late forties whose work has given him intimate knowledge of many religious men and women from different congregations and of the Catholic Church in general.

Many superiors are wanting things to move away from the past, but the issue is broader than religious life. In many ways, religious life can only be a reflection of church structure. I still feel there's a fairly high level of very conservative feeling in the church and in religious life. This does not encourage religious to try new ventures or to take risks that might fail. Old structures are still dying. While these slow changes are good for older religious—it's not fair to expect them to adopt radically new ideas—I fear that slow change will discourage religious from wanting something different because they won't have an opportunity of doing it. I've seen recent figures that show people joining the priesthood and religious life are scoring high on conservative personality factors. This combination of factors, together with the overall image religious life has in Australia, means that the adventurous, gifted young people with ideas do not see religious life as a structure within which to work and develop. Many young people tell me they're looking for a new kind of community, not that of the present religious life.

A lot of new constitutions have lovely language and ideas and some religious have moved from large communities to small groups in nice Jennings' houses well set up, but young religious are still experiencing much the same kind of community life in them and so are leaving. It's debatable whether the old and new in one province, let alone in one community, can exist together. If they can't, we'll find splinter-groups being a source of religious life in the future.

More than one priest spoke of changes in community life as being surface ones. 'There has been no real conversion,' said one in his thirties, while another with his own vision of community is frustrated by an inability to create real fundamental changes. He said: 'We come together because the structure demands it, not for each other or for God. We pray together only because we should.' A priest in his early sixties deliberately challenges his community by questioning why things are done or not done. 'Some men', he commented, 'can intellectually grasp what is meant by change, but fail to integrate them in themselves.' Another priest doubts that religious life will develop within existing structures: 'We're trying to force new wine into old wineskins. The best fellows are killing themselves trying to change, but basically can't.'

Conclusion

Religious priests seem to be experiencing more tension within their communities than are brothers. Some priests are happy with their community style, while a number are concerned that the energy behind the initial changes undertaken after Vatican II is lessening or, in some cases, religious are consciously halting or reversing the development of change. Overall, community life does not appear to be the issue with brothers as it is with priests and sisters. Brothers have a more unified and less intense view of community. They do not talk about a community being a sign, nor about the need to form small communities in ordinary houses among lay people. A few brothers are living in such communities, but it is not an issue with them: the change was a natural consequence of their ministry.

Both old and young brothers testified that, despite weaknesses in their community life, 'at rock bottom', as a brother in his thirties said, 'the brothers are there behind me'. They look for and do feel they have community support, if not within their local community then within their congregation as a whole. A young brother in his twenties spoke about his appreciation for his community: 'It is a great feeling to know you are not charging through life on your own.'

Of the three groups, religious women have the highest expectations of community. A good proportion, indeed, are overly concerned with the internal functioning of their local community and largely depend on it to fulfil their sociological and emotional needs. Their history is mainly responsible for this attitude. Traditionally, religious women stayed within enclosure walls. Necessarily, they became involved in what happened within them. Gradually, from about 1970, hitherto rigid internal structures and timetables tended to be abolished in most congregations, the emphasis on the good of the congregation as a whole shifted to the good of the individual, and religious women were able to leave their convents to mingle more freely with the laity. Nevertheless, many religious women have maintained their emphasis on life in community. The increasing number of elderly sisters and the lack of younger ones contribute to the emphasis. There are also some sisters, perhaps a growing number, who want a certain conformity and uniformity so that the community as a group can retain control of its members. Still caught in traditional thinking, the majority do not believe that social, political or environmental issues are their concern. These issues belong to lay people. Theirs are spiritual, and connected with their traditional and parish ministries. A minority of religious women are struggling to create a new pattern of religious community. This new pattern arises from what they see as their ministry. For them, the once common goal—to love God and to save souls for the kingdom—has been widened to include working for human development and the improvement of society in the here-and-now. Inevitably, this new attitude and approach to ministry will create new shapes of religious communities.

Ministry 6

Sisters

Catholic buildings of stone and brick dominate many small Australian towns, an example of which is Cooma. One drives down into the valley and, through sheer size and position, the Catholic convent draws all eyes towards it. Built in the early 1880s for a teaching congregation of sisters, it typifies what was then happening in the history of Catholic Australians. The bishops had made their stand against the government: from their flocks' resources they would provide Catholic children with a Catholic education so that they would not be tainted by what the bishops saw as a completely secular education. Convents and monasteries were built to accommodate religious sisters and brothers, drawn largely from Ireland, to be the teachers in the new schools. Great stone buildings dominating houses and shops were like gauntlets thrown down before those not of the Catholic faith: Catholics could and would stand alone to preserve the faith of their children.

These buildings were not often solely for the private use of religious. Within them were housed the boarders, children from distant country areas; and school classes were usually conducted in rooms or on verandas. In contrast, there were other religious living in small cottages, identical with their neighbours. Of necessity, their lives were more informal than those in large buildings, and they mingled easily among the people. The bishops had themselves determined the needs of Australian Catholics and were responsible for the influx of teaching congregations into Australia, in the belief that, if children were taught what was good, they would do it and be saved. The main thrust of Catholic energy was to go into the building and maintenance of schools. Catholics not so enthusiastic about sending their children to schools for which they had to pay were often threatened with hell and damnation: in some dioceses, even in the fourth decade of the twentieth century, parents of children in state schools were refused the sacraments.

Before Vatican II the great majority of religious sisters and brothers knew—and the laity knew—they were needed in a very basic way in schools: there was no finance for lay teachers. There was hardly enough money to support the religious. Like the ninety-year-old sister quoted in the last chapter, a forty-seven-year-old sister recalled that, when the parish priest (as owner of the school) told the sisters he had to keep school fees for the maintenance of the school itself, and was unable to afford stipends for them, they gave private lessons in music and art of speech to support themselves. People gave what assistance they could: meat came from nearby properties; eggs and vegetables were constant offerings from townsfolk. For the majority of Catholics, a religious was one who taught in schools and they accorded her or him respect and status.

In 1986, of the 100 sisters interviewed, twenty-four were still working in the schools and forty-six had spent most of their religious life in the schools. Thus, 70 per cent in this study are associated with Catholic schools. Inevitably, the teaching congregation geared itself to the needs of the school institution, and the needs of the individual religious were usually subordinate. Because of the demand for religious teachers, many young women entering a congregation had no option in ministry. A sixty-year-old Irish sister said she had never wanted to be a teacher: 'I wanted to be a nurse. But the need for teachers was great when I arrived in Australia, so on my arrival I was just told to teach.' The same pressure forced a forty-five-year-old sister into teaching: 'In the early 1960s there was an influx of children into schools, so naturally every sister had to teach. It was blind obedience all right. I just fell into the groove.'

Older sisters spoke of long, arduous hours of work in their school experiences. A seventy-three-year-old sister had once taught ninety pupils in one class while she was bursar of a community of twenty sisters, which duty often meant she cooked the main meal for them after school. After forty years of teaching, another sister of the same age had a nervous and physical breakdown from overwork and pressure. Two sisters in their late fifties had both taught composite groups of four classes and given typing and shorthand lessons after school hours, one for thirteen consecutive years.

Occasionally over-activity was self-induced. A sister in her late forties admitted:

I have learnt that much of my ministry has come out of my own needs. I'd exhaust myself in my work and a good friend used to say to me, 'What are you getting out of it?' It took me a long time to realise I was getting reassurance that I was a success as a sister. Maybe some of our parish programmes are designed to answer our needs, not the needs of the people.

With no finance to pay lay teachers to replace them while they studied, many sisters received no formal training as teachers and learnt on the job. A sister in her seventies remembered getting help from an old sister in charge of the infants school: 'All the tricks I picked up from her were later introduced into the system and became fashionable.' A fifty-nine-year-old sister with no teacher training was for some years teacher, principal and superior of a community of fourteen. This was in the early 1970s, when changes in religious life were making their impact: 'I found it difficult to balance my three roles—principal, teacher, superior—especially as there was no longer a clear definition of the role of superior.' It is easy to think of the implications for the sisters when the same person, under great pressure, was in charge of both school and community. From about 1960, however, it was far more common for sisters to acquire teacher's certificates or university degrees. Some congregations developed a policy of ensuring full professional training for all sisters once they made their first profession of vows, but even as late as 1967, not all sisters were trained as a matter of course. A forty-one-year-old sister who had no training said: 'I still look upon myself as a second-rate teacher.' Some, for example a seventy-year-old, considered themselves privileged if they were permitted to study part-time while teaching in the schools.

Success in the schools was measured by the results in public examinations. A seventy-two-year-old sister remembered teaching the top grade in primary school: 'The children had to sit for an entrance examination to the secondary school, and if I got a big percentage passing the examination, I felt I had done good work and that the children were being helped to move up in life.' Pressure to achieve success had other results. A sixty-two-year-old Irish sister regretted that she had been too strict with the children she taught, but 'the parents were making sacrifices to pay fees to send them to a Catholic school so I had to make sure the children did well'.

Because the majority of congregations were semi-monastic before Vatican II, sisters were usually not permitted or encouraged to visit families of their pupils. A few congregations, however, carried their ministry directly into homes. One eighty-year-old sister loved teaching and fondly recalled visiting parents of her pupils:

> I used to walk along many a bush track to come to a little home by the side of a creek. There'd be a little hessian bag at the door for a mat. On the back of a couple of chairs there'd be a possum skin or a sheepskin to rest against. There was always a big kettle swinging over the fire and the first thing the mother would do was to make me a cup of tea.

A ninety-year-old sister remembered her Sunday's activities:

> In the morning we'd visit the hospital and old people's homes, and very often we would have the happiness of getting someone back into the church. Then by 2 p.m. there wouldn't be a sister left in the house. We would all be out, two by two, teaching in various Sunday schools.

Many sisters who had had no teacher training and/or no real desire to teach moved out of the schools when government funding increased and change of ministry became more acceptable within congregations. This trend was noticeable and usually frowned upon in the late 1970s, but accepted as the norm in the 1980s. One reason for the exodus from schools was the pressure on sisters to gain or update their teacher's certificate. This was the case for a fifty-five-year-old sister who moved out of teaching three years ago; at her age she felt that, although she loved teaching, it was not worth while to update her training.

Lack of formal training, however, was not inevitably an impediment, as the story of an energetic seventy-eight-year-old sister revealed. Untrained, she taught successfully for forty years before taking charge of a library in a Catholic Teachers' College, again without formal training for the job. By the time she left the library she had built it up so successfully that there were fourteen people on the staff: 'I made sure to get the right ones for the right places.' She then moved into a group of women organising parish activities especially for the handicapped.

In some cases the move to a second ministry is gradual. Five sisters continue to teach on a part-time basis as they begin working in the parish. Others move directly into new ministries, sometimes after retraining for their new work. Others are not so effectively changing ministries. There is a large number of sisters from their mid-fifties to mid-sixties who are healthy, energetic, eager for work and yet unable to find an appropriate ministry for which they will be paid a stipend. Many in this age-group are also anxious about what they will do after retirement from their very active ministries. It does not appear that Australian bishops are as interested as were their predecessors to tap this source of dedicated, experienced women. On the other hand, religious congregations may be depending too much on bishops: the majority are still seeking the explicit approval and support of bishops and/or priests before moving into a new geographical area or a new ministry. In the future, religious congregations may have to project more actively and visibly an independent, prophetic role of leadership, which tradition in other countries has consistently attributed to them. Such a role of leadership will of necessity lead them in new directions.

Sisters under fifty years are questioning their role in schools, especially as more and more lay teachers replace them. They no longer see themselves, a forty-six-year-old sister explained, as 'saviours of the school', although a forty-two-year-old sister believes that 'we still have something very valuable to offer in schools'. As a fifty-year-old sister said: 'A lot of our Catholic traditions can be lost if there aren't religious in a supportive role with lay principals during these years.' But the values of a Catholic school thirty years ago are not those of today. Now the only religious on the staff, a forty-two-year-old sister once taught

in a school where these might be watered down or where other values are put forward. To be a lone person pushing for certain values is difficult. Lay teachers are understandably interested in seeking higher positions for money or status. That changes the ethos of the school.

A forty-eight-year-old sister finds the school 'a pretty tough experience as it is a highly systematised group of people. I have to be fairly assertive to maintain what I believe are the principal goals of the school.' Principal of a secondary school for six years, a thirty-nine-year-old sister presented another viewpoint:

> Lay teachers are really challenging us to clarify what we understand by Catholic school and Catholic education and sometimes we have been too narrow about that. As sisters, we used to think it meant keeping the Catholic culture intact. To me, now, it is much broader than that. It has been purifying for us sisters to be working with lay teachers and to find their reaction to us. We've had to tone down some things that were in our tradition; we've had to broaden and recognise some of our weaknesses.

Five years ago a thirty-six-year-old principal saw great value in her work in a secondary school, but now questions it:

> I believe in theory in the power of education to transform people's minds and attitudes and therefore, hopefully, the society in which they live. I feel now that secondary education is so constrained that it is impossible to break through all the negative aspects of the system to help in the transformation process. As principal today I am trying to salvage the whole process of Catholic education, and I just don't think it will work. In terms of social analysis, we are so aligned with the power blocs in society and with all those supporting forces of the power blocs that we can't make changes. We are too caught up with maintaining the structure. When my term of office ends, I will leave the school.

Other sisters are questioning the purpose of education. The main issue for a forty-one-year-old sister is how effective one or two religious can be in a school, especially as fewer sisters are willing to take on the role of principal:

> It is more and more difficult to make them thoroughly Christian schools. We find the educational system very constricting. Whereas we would see our role as educating the whole person, we seem to

be forced to bow to the system of scores and ratings.

A thirty-four-year-old sister supported her view:

> I don't think religious fit into the rat race in the school system: there is always a struggle to see who gets the best results. I didn't get professed in religious life to be competitive in secular subjects.

A forty-three-year-old sister who intends remaining in the school is not placing her emphasis on examination results: 'My fundamental aim is to help children grow and develop as persons, to make them feel confident in what they are learning and in themselves.'

Ten sisters in this study are still working as nurses, and seven were once nurses, so 17 per cent of the interviewees are or have been associated with nursing. They, like religious teachers, once experienced great pressures in maintaining large institutions. A sixty-five-year-old nurse said she worked in a hospital seven days a week and was on call every night for six years. Hers was not an unique case. A seventy-three-year-old sister recalled that she was often on night duty for six consecutive weeks, then on day duty as well as being on call during the night: 'There wasn't a night free from a call.' Another nurse in her early sixties said that she used to rise at 5 a.m. for prayers and retire at 10 p.m. with time off only for meals:

> I have never regretted the hard work, but I very much regret that I was told to exempt myself from community prayers in order to work. I also regret that I followed instructions to repress my feelings for the patients and their families.

Like their teaching sisters, those who nursed had a certain status among the Catholic people. This sometimes had an effect on them. A seventy-eight-year-old sister ruefully said:

> We used to think that because we were sisters, whether we were qualified or not, we were just a little superior to those with whom we were working. I've found since that some of those people, especially nurses who were fully trained and more experienced than we were, had to suffer through our sense of superiority.

116

A fifty-year-old sister appreciates that she has worked in a public hospital as well as in one managed by her congregation:

> When I worked in our own hospital the lay staff treated me carefully and with great respect; they never criticised the hospital or its management in front of me. They were naturally afraid of losing their jobs. When I worked in a nearby public hospital, the staff treated me as one of themselves. They were not frightened to give negative criticism of our hospital. I felt I was living in a real world where before I was in a ghetto.

Younger sisters are giving more time for relationships with patients. A thirty-six-year-old nurse tries to be a support person for mothers for whom she cares: 'I find myself drawn to that kind of caring and I would like to move into counselling. I'd like a closer interaction with people.' The desire for a more personal caring of the individual is drawing younger religious from nursing in the institutional hospital. A sister in her late thirties nursed in a hospital for fourteen years before doing home nursing. She said: 'I never really settled when I returned to the hospital. That nursing experience brought me into the community and I saw how people lived and struggled in their homes. So I returned to home nursing.' Younger sisters are not all intending to remain as nurses in hospitals. A thirty-five-year-old nurse said she loved her work but, 'I have a feeling that, after about five years, I will be doing other work'.

Sisters are therefore moving out of their traditional ministry in school and hospital. Those who have moved out or who intend to do so in the near future would mostly support a forty-seven-year-old nursing sister when she categorically stated that ministry must come out of very obvious need, and to find that need one has to listen carefully to people. The results of this search have reshaped religious life for a number of sisters and, in some cases, have created difficulties within congregations. A forty-four-year-old sister, now living and working with three other sisters in a poor suburb, spoke of reactions from her neighbours and from the sisters in traditional convents:

> We live in a house that can't be distinguished from the others in the street. We have merged into the local community of people

and yet we are very visible for that reason—it is a strange paradox, but that's the way it is. When the neighbours are in difficulties, we're the people they come to, because we are trusted, we're OK people. It's not a good way of achieving great things if you are into the numbers game. It's very much a being thing rather than a doing. We hope we are seen as people who really care, who are to be trusted and have a lot to offer. The sisters living in big institutions find it hard to understand what we're doing. They'd understand if you told them you had eighty girls under your roof and you were caring for them. What we are doing is beyond their experience.

This sister has the support of three other sisters living and working with her, but, when a sister moves into social welfare work as an individual and still lives in the traditional convent, she has to cope with many aspects of loneliness. Although she found teaching rewarding, a thirty-year-old sister moved into parish work, believing that the people there needed her more. She said: 'I know some sisters are disappointed at my change. They have the idea that those who work in the parish are looking for a slack job.' A sixty-year-old sister moved into social welfare because she saw a great need in this area. She said:

When I first began welfare work, I felt very isolated, very unsupported. Once, after spending four hours talking to a would-be suicide, I went back to the convent and saw a row of heads in front of *The Sullivans* on television. I knew I would be hushed if I spoke. Someone said, 'There's salad for you in the frig.' It's better now. I'm more confident in my work, and I have thirty wonderful parishioners who work with me as volunteers, and they support me. I don't look so much to my community for support now.

Sisters undertaking social welfare or similar work realise that some in their congregations cannot understand why they have undertaken such work. Usually, as a forty-eight-year-old sister commented, 'We try not to alienate those who are locked into the world of the 1940s.' Some, indeed, find little support from the church. A fifty-seven-year-old sister living with two others in an ordinary house in a developing suburb learnt this the hard way.

I don't get spoken or demonstrated support from the established church in this area, but my religious superiors have confidence in what I am doing. The church does not seem aware that there are people not up to the stage of going to Mass. They first need to be friends with others, to know a human being who will smile and listen to them. Community development—that is what I am on about. They were first frightened of me and I had to learn to speak their language and to dress casually; for example, I no longer wear stockings. I join action groups urging the local council to do things for the people and I doorknock to get supporters. I aim to be a helping person without any religious distinction and to be in a supportive rather than a leadership role. Sometimes I get so tired, emotionally and physically, that I pretend I am not at home when someone knocks, because I could do damage to the other person when I'm like that.

A fifty-year-old sister spoke for others presently engaged in internal administration:

Authority roles are more nebulous today. I'm not too certain of what my role as provincial councillor is when we are encouraging communities to be more autonomous. I also feel torn between the varying expectations of sisters, the structures of the present and how I would personally like to operate in my position. Anyone in authority today must experience these difficulties.

Eight sisters participating in this study are fully retired; ten, semi-retired, are visiting people in their parishes. The work of other sisters includes lecturing in colleges, in religious education centres, to adults within parish groups; caring for unmarried pregnant girls; teaching preschool and handicapped children; and helping Aborigines. A fifty-two-year-old sister explained her ministry, which she shares with another:

When I was school principal, I found it took very little communication for mothers to cry, saying they were at the end of their rope, but if only they could get a break, they could cope. There was nothing for them at a reasonable price. So we established this house for five or six mothers. They stay ten days and we help them become spiritually, emotionally and physically refreshed.

There is always, she said, a waiting list.

Three sisters are on Motor Mission in the outback. They travel from parish to parish or from home to home during the week, usually returning to their community at the weekend or midweek. A fifty-eight-year-old sister is in charge of religious education in twenty-four state schools. She travels over eight hundred kilometres each week. Another sister, sixty-four years old, has been on Motor Mission for twenty years. She now travels seven hundred kilometres a week where before she had travelled over one thousand. She feels she is with the spiritually poor: 'The only contact the parents have with the church is when I visit and teach their children.'

Eleven sisters in this study are engaged in full-time parish work. Their ages range from thirty-seven to sixty-three years. They, like their sisters in social welfare, often feel that the members of their community do not really know what they are doing, so they are looking for challenge and support from lay people. The work in the parish varies: older sisters tend to distribute holy communion, visit the ill and elderly and generally help the parish priest; others are responsible for religious education in one or more parishes. A forty-year-old sister is enthusiastic about her work: 'It has opened up for me a much broader scene than teaching could provide. I'm learning how people live.' A sixty-two-year-old sister who had domestic duties within the convent for forty years began working in a parish at the request of the parish priest: 'Since then, over four years ago, I have come alive in myself. I feel worthwhile in my work with the poor. They accept me.' A parish worker, as a sixty-six-year-old sister explained, tends to experience problems when a new man replaces the parish priest who originally employed her.

Until and beyond the 1960s the religious sister was seen as belonging either to the school or to the hospital. She wore black or brown medieval clothing and veil, and rarely moved out of her convent; and when she did, it was in company with another sister. Her life was rigidly organised into a daily pattern of work and prayer. She was sure of her role and place in the church. By 1986 the religious sister was no longer anonymous and a stereotype. With support from her major superiors, she has assessed her value in the old role in the institutional ministry and has made her decision to continue within it for a limited period or to begin a more pastoral/spiritual ministry within it or, after ascertaining the needs of a group of people, to begin a new ministry for them. Decision to move from an institutional ministry is not lightly taken. One principal, for example, hopes she will eventually take on another ministry:

> I feel very strongly, however, about acting responsibly in the way we go out of schools. We have to make sure that lay people are ready to take over administrative positions. Moreover, if I move out it will not be because I want to do my own thing; it would have to be the result of my congregation's reflection on the priority of needs. We would have to reflect and make a decision together.

With changes in ministry comes insecurity of employment for the sister and, eventually, financial insecurity for the congregation. Working within school and hospital, sisters were always sure of a job, even if, in latter years, as a fifty-five-year-old nurse pointed out, the job was one created for her as a religious. Once the sister leaves the institution run by her congregation or the Catholic Education Office, she is not certain of receiving a stipend; the sister in the parish rarely receives a full stipend. Such insecurity has not deterred the sisters. A forty-seven-year-old said:

> What I really think we have to do is to get out of the rut of the embedded ministry that our church had given us in the past and to see with creativity where the real needs are now and go out to meet them with courage rather than with the security of an accepted ministry from middle and upper class Catholics.

The trend is very clear. The majority of sisters want to move out from institutions that lay people are well qualified to manage. They wish to become more involved in the spiritual formation of children and especially of adults. As a thirty-nine-year-old sister remarked: 'It is time for religious to move explicity into the area of faith development.' They wish to move out to people who need them instead of expecting people to come to them to be told their needs. Many wish to be indistinguishable in dress and housing from those they help. They wish to be more involved in a very caring way with the daily life and concerns of the ordinary person. And they know they will receive as much as they give.

Brothers

Of brothers interviewed, 92 per cent are engaged in school ministry, and they believe that the majority of brothers will remain in education. As one said: 'We still have the desire to work together at a particular ministry and not to fragment into other work.' 'The example of a community with four brothers doing four different jobs', said a brother in his forties, 'is a long way down the track for us.' Of the remaining brothers, one is bursar of a large community, the other is involved in social work. All brothers felt supported by their communities. Referring to the past, one brother said wryly: 'The old work ethic survived a long time. The attitude of your community depended a lot on how you performed. If I hadn't been successful, maybe I wouldn't have had as much support.'

A brother in his seventies recalled that in his younger days a brother was expected to be an 'all rounder' in teaching. Extra study was not usual, sometimes it was discouraged. Change came in the 1950s.

These young fellows began to come out with their university degrees and wouldn't teach chemistry because they hadn't done honours in chemistry. I began to sit up and realise I would remain a plug, so, at about thirty-five years of age, I decided to become a specialist too.

After studying some years part-time, he was told he would be given a year's full-time study to complete his second degree, but when the time came, 'they said they wanted teachers', so he never finished this degree. Brothers now appear to take it for granted that extra study is essential, even after the completion of their first degree.

Brothers had once placed their emphasis on successful examination results. 'You taught like a thrashing machine,' said one in his early forties, 'with the firm belief that if you didn't, no one else would. You had an obligation to the kids to lift them above where they were.' Without jeopardising examination results, the emphasis has shifted. A brother in his sixties had this to say:

> Earlier I was looking for academic success. I would be happier now to work with boys who can improve only a little bit. I don't see it as a case of making them better people, but a case where I can contribute to what is already happening in them.

A brother in his forties said: 'I like to find the particular needs of a kid and help him there.' Another brother commented: 'I want to pass on my enthusiasm and interest in my subjects. When it's appropriate, I use the study to raise philosophical questions.' Several brothers work within a boarding school. One, in his late twenties, said: 'The influence of the religious is most marked among the boarders. There we have a chance to come close to the kids, and I count it a real privilege to share time with them.'

Two brothers are working outside the normal school situation. One in his late thirties initiated a new programme within his school. 'I worked with the lower stream of kids, and I wanted to make their education as relevant and wholesome as possible. Then unemployment rose and something else had to be done.' In his new course, his boys are treated more like employees, clocking in and out for the day. Using the trades to teach them self-reliance and the ability to work together as a team, he arranges for the boys to work one day a week with tradesmen and to give community service for half a day. 'It's very, very worthwhile,' he said.

Speaking about his involvement with the handicapped, a brother in his thirties remarked:

> In the localised church our work for disabled people becomes a very dynamic sign of how we regard quality of life and the need to maintain and improve it. That's what we're on about. We also want to be a voice for the voiceless.

Only one brother was unenthusiastic about his work of teaching and only one disenchanted with the Catholic school system. The latter's comment was:

It is increasingly evident that, if Catholic schools were once centres of spirituality in the past, they aren't now. They are too divorced from reality. Parents depend completely on the school for religious input for children, whereas it has to be a combination of school, family and church community.

He and another brother in his seventies work, but not together, with Aborigines. Both have found it difficult to adapt to another culture, but see their work as valuable. The older brother admitted: 'It's frustrating work. I can't chalk up results as I used to do. Here I see myself accompanying a people, helping them to work out their vision for the future and their goals.'

Brothers in clerical congregations originally concentrated on internal and mainly domestic chores. Changes for them, according to one in his late forties, came naturally: 'More priests were opting out of schools, so superiors looked for people to fill gaps and saw this great horde of brothers really wasting time doing things for which they could employ lay people.' His story is not atypical. Over the years he had worked as tailor, school infirmarian, bursar, sports master, dormitory master with emphasis on pastoral care, and part-time teacher before he took up his present position as assistant headmaster. 'In thirteen years', he said, with justifiable pride, 'I went from being a cleaner of toilets to assistant head-master.' Within brothers' congregations there had been non-teaching members. These, too, have altered course. One such brother in his fifties had been cook, farmer, school maintenance man and cleaner before teaching religious education and acting as counsellor in his position as dormitory master. For some years he has also been superior of his community. Again, his story is that of others.

As much as possible, brothers have concentrated their personnel in administrative positions within schools. All the principals interviewed enjoy their role, although one in his mid-thirties admitted: 'I feel scared at times when I think about the power I have over other lives and the challenge to use it for their benefit. It's a great opportunity to support and encourage others.'

One in his forties said of his work as principal:

Nobody else could do it quite as I do it. It's part of the charism of being a brother and part of my individual thing — a gift — together with the skills of relating to people that I've gained over the years.

One brother, preferring classroom teaching to his position as principal, neatly solved his problem by developing a system of delegation whereby he releases himself for some teaching each week.

Brothers enjoy a high degree of self-confidence in their ministry. According to a young brother, they see their presence in the school 'as a countersign to kids of a lot of things society demands, for example, permissiveness. Judging from the number who return to say "Hello", they appreciate us in the schools.' Belief in their own value has meant an ease in acceptance of the increasing number of lay people on their teaching staff. Brothers voiced positive attitudes towards lay teachers and assumed a responsibility towards them since they were working in Catholic schools originally established by their congregations.

> We realise [said one principal] that we need the expertise and talents of people other than ourselves, so we draw them into our work. This, of course, commits us to ensuring that they believe in and uphold our philosophy. We see this as a special ministry because they are the people who will, in the future, maintain and express the charism of our congregation.

Brothers are realising that their ageing congregations, with less intake and some brothers thinking of moving into ministries other than that of the school, have fewer potential administrators at a time when Catholic lay teachers are increasing, especially those interested in administrative positions. One brother offered his views:

> We haven't yet sufficient lay people well trained and prepared to take on the role of principal. We did have a couple of lay principals, and they didn't last long. We need not only to train but also to build up a system of support for these people . . . Our congregation has put in a few lay deputy principals and in four or six years they will be ready to be principals. In this time we have

to break down the prevalent thinking among parents that brother does the job best.

From his own experience, a principal realises one difficulty of a lay principal: 'With only one brother on my staff I at first felt that I had only one real supporter, one to confide in. My isolation as principal made me more aware of a lay principal's difficulty in this area.'

The number of lay teachers has created new problems. A brother explained that in earlier years 'the brothers had a stacked house at staff meetings and the lay teachers had little influence or say. Today there may only be a couple of brothers on a staff of forty or fifty.' They have had to learn to work harder at creating group support and seeing lay teachers as equals. One brother had difficulty in adjusting: 'One of my main reasons for entering religious life was to teach among brothers. I had to re-think my vocation when I joined a large staff of lay teachers.' Brothers are sometimes moved for community reasons and then have to take available positions within the school, even if the subjects or classes are not of their choice. To help in such a case, one principal annually rotates classes and subjects among his teachers as much as possible.

Priests

Of the priests interviewed, twelve were in parishes (of these, four had taught in schools for many years), five were still in schools, three in formation or renewal work, and the remaining five concentrated on adult education or media work. When speaking of his ministry, not one mentioned that it included offering Mass or giving sacraments. One point, however, emerged strongly. Wherever they worked, the majority of priests emphasised the importance of availability and of being with people in their daily lives. For this latter reason, one priest, while teaching, had extended his work by providing temporary shelter for homeless families. 'This', he said, 'sparked off a lot of things I wanted to express in my priesthood. I felt closer to the ordinariness of people's lives.'

Most priests felt that schools, with their curriculum and sporting demands, limited the pastoral potential of priests.

126

Only two held the opposite view. One of these was a principal in his mid-thirties who admits enjoying his position as superior and principal, but he too recently felt the need to become more involved in spiritual areas: 'I now have a strong commitment to prayer, to the God side of my religious vocation.' Two priests wish to continue within the school system, but not as teachers. One in his thirties explained his ideas:

> It is an uphill battle to humanise the school system. I've been trying for three years to introduce a pastoral care programme, and I've been given the go-ahead for next year. This is where we should be at, giving people confidence to communicate with each other.

The other, in his late fifties, would like to see someone within the school system with no other commitment than to be totally available to any student who wished to talk to him: 'It would help to break down the impersonality of a large school.' He himself made a point of having his lunch in the playground so that he could walk around and talk to the boys: 'If I didn't, the only time I'd meet them would be when they came to me for discipline. That's no way to make relationships.'

Recently moved from the school to the parish, a priest in his early seventies said:

> I am closer to people now, and it's given me a new lease of life. I believe it is the ordinary everyday conversation with people that is just as important as trying to teach them about the Catholic Church. I like to see them talking to each other in church because that shows they're friendly with each other and at home in the church and with the priest.

He has encouraged young people to go in their social groups to Mass and they have responded well.

A few priests also spoke of innovations needed within existing parish structures. One said:

> The emphasis has been too long on the parish priest, whereas it should be on the people. They have to take a more active, responsible part. There's a tremendous lot of energy, good will and talent waiting to be encouraged.

Another priest in his thirties also wants priests to move out of their dominant role: 'People are realising they too have a ministry in this church and parish and this is already having temendous repercussions.' He believes priests should be trained to give guidance in the new directions parishes will take. A parish priest welcomed a recent demand from the laity for their diocese to establish its own adult education programme.

Priests are already concentrating on working with Catholics no longer attending church. One in his thirties confessed: 'I felt very guilty about the fact that the poor never feel at home in the church, not only the physically poor but the big sinners.' So, with four lay volunteers, he is working among the unchurched and the unemployed youth. Another priest sees a real challenge in working with migrants, especially in the area of healing breaches caused by misunderstanding between the original migrants and their Australian children and grandchildren.

Two priests lived in monasteries to which people come for retreats, recollection days and spiritual guidance. They were occasionally involved in mission work to parishes, but that work, admitted one, does not belong to the future. The first priest, a contemplative in his forties, was content to remain within his monastery:

> The life itself is the main emphasis, it is not the work. In the end there comes a time when you have to put down roots and accept the limitations of a particular situation, whether it is in married life or religious life. That kind of stability has its own developing process of mechanisms, so it's loss in one way, gain in another.

The second, a man in his early sixties, was very concerned that the church was irrelevant to the people in the street, the ones, as he said, really carrying the burden of today's society. His dream is to become involved in a large community consisting of married and single men and women, people of all religions including non-Christian peoples. In his opinion such a mixed interaction would produce great riches:

> If we remain living in a one sex institution and apart from other religions then we're not really being fed the Gospel. We need more

than pious words. We haven't sufficiently stressed that to be fully Christian is to be fully human.

Conclusion

To be fully Christian is to be fully human: this is the theme underlying revolutionary changes in the ministry of religious in recent years. In the past the greater proportion of religious sisters and brothers were in schools, and from many angles it was a narrow area of ministry among young Catholics under eighteen years of age with little effective outreach to Catholic adults, let alone non-Catholics. Today this is no longer true: in the Sydney archdiocese in 1986, for example, the official number of religious in regional schools was 5.1 per cent of the total teaching staff. Qualified lay people have largely replaced religious in the schools, thus freeing religious to direct their personnel and resources towards adults and to new areas of ministry. Among religious men and women a growing and marked emphasis on the value of personal contact with adults, an open acknowledgement of the humanity of a person and of that person's complex history shaping his/her life style, attitudes and spiritual values have led to greater empathy and friendliness between religious and laity. For many religious, therefore, ministry has become a two-way street.

Australian society 7

Positive changes

Sisters

I asked all religious interviewed if they saw anything happening within Australian society that was helping Australians become better human beings. Of the sisters interviewed, 15 per cent admitted a lack of knowledge on the topic, and, despite a rewording of the question to emphasise that we were looking at the total Australian scene, 28 per cent of sisters spoke only of movements within the Catholic Church: the Antioch movement for youth, marriage encounter groups and prayer groups, both charismatic and non-charismatic, were the main ones mentioned. Another 19 per cent first spoke about church movements, then, after the rewording of the question, talked about positive happenings within society as a whole. The remaining 38 per cent of sisters spoke directly and immediately to the question. A few sisters acknowledged the good achieved by non-Catholic churches and religious sects. A seventy-four-year-old sister commented: 'Groups like the Ananda Marga turn me off, but they are striving for something. Everybody is looking for truth, even if they are looking the wrong direction.' Another sister, also in her seventies, was delighted at the growing unity of churches:

> In my parish, three clergymen, one each from the Uniting Church, the Anglican and the Catholic, hold united prayer meetings weekly during Lent, rotating the meetings in the three churches. When the Anglicans have a floral festival, they send a special invitation to the sisters, and they greet us warmly when we attend. I think God is there in all that.

The most important positive development among Australians was seen to be that in appreciative awareness, particularly in areas where formerly extremely prejudiced views were held. A forty-two-year-old sister was one of those who saw Australian writers and poets helping in this development. She said:

> A. D. Hope is looking at and questioning our society, and he is

132

asking us to do the same. Patrick White is helping Australians to become more aware of themselves and of the nature of their relationships with each other. God is in that growth of awareness and understanding of what people should be about.

She added: 'Ted Kennedy [a Catholic priest working with Aborigines in Redfern] is an Australian prophet, and he is very powerful in his statements about what the church could be doing in society.'

Australians are becoming more aware of the beauty within other cultures and quicker to accept cultural differences within their society. One sister in her late forties remembered a crowd on a recent Australia Day watching a Greek group dancing in the streets. Some onlookers were upset that Greeks would celebrate as Greeks on Australia Day, but others laughed, saying: 'Well, that's the Greek-Australians for you.' More than one sister witnessed to this growing appreciation of other cultures. A seventy-three-year-old sister said: 'Acceptance of ethnic minorities within our society shows that Australians are reaching out beyond selfishness. It is a sign of God moving because one learns such a lot from these people.' She sees this acceptance arising from compassion and great caring for underprivileged minorities.

Minorities include the Aboriginal people, who are beginning to express a greater sense of their own dignity and worth. Sisters believe sensitivity and respect for Aborigines and for their claim to land rights are growing, although several commented that an emphasis on militancy in Australian society, especially in the industrial arena, relegates such respect to pockets of interest. However, according to a forty-eight-year-old sister, these pockets of interest are a growing force:

There are people very socially concerned, and they know that, to be effective, they have to change the political arena, and we have seen evidence of that over the last ten years. Groups such as Action for World Development and Community Aid Abroad are viable and effective and continually putting pressure on governments. They are well informed, and that is an important start. I have met a number of retired men who now give themselves to studying certain areas, for example, Aboriginal welfare, the law or aspects of justice connected with local government.

Sisters were enthusiastic about the growing support for peace, a nuclear free society and social justice for all. As one sister in her thirties remarked: 'Religion is not separated from the world. It is in the world. There is a more natural approach to life today: we are finding God in the secular and the wholeness of truth in just ordinary living.' A ninety-one-year-old-sister supports this belief:

There are a lot of good things in Australian society leading people to God, even though they do not do these things with God in their minds. They are doing what Christ himself would do if he were in their place. Look, for example, at the help the Australian Government has given to boat people from Vietnam and to migrants in general.

Sisters recognise the changing attitudes within Government. One in her late thirties commented:

You have someone like Bob Hawke talking about the importance of reconciliation, of unity, of working together. These are Gospel values. They are not being achieved fully, but we are working on them. God's presence is in that. Moreover, there is a real consciousness of the feminine, and there is a movement away from relating in a dominating way. We are slowly moving from a patriarchal, authoritarian society. We are also breaking down so many barriers between different religions. I'm a great believer in Teilhard de Chardin's understanding of evolution, and it's happening here.

A seventy-one-year-old sister spoke about

a humane and Christian presence in parliament led by the vocal minority. The Australian Council of Social Services cries out in the ears of the powerful for the poor and marginalised. There are voluntary workers spending countless hours working to make this world a better place for everybody, not just for a few.

More groups, according to a forty-year-old sister, are standing beside the disadvantaged and the elderly in the name of justice.

134

A sister in her late fifties was only one who saw in society a search for small community groups: 'Everywhere I go I find people saying that they must set up some structures for meeting one another.' The search for community appears widespread. A forty-two-year-old sister said:

> I live in an ordinary suburb with non-churchgoers, and I see the Spirit leading them into community groups to do things together. All the ministers in the area meet to form an ecumenical justice group. There is a whole bonding of a human community here: they have formed a fruit co-operative, a housing group to help people with temporary rent difficulties, a food group and a mothers' group for child-minding services.

Many tributes were paid to the goodness of non-church people. One came from a thirty-four-year-old sister: 'People I know have no religion as such, but they believe in giving others a fair go no matter who they are.' One sister declared: 'I see a movement away from the established church in Australian society, and yet I don't equate that with a movement away from God. A lot of people have a sense of God.'

A sister in her mid-thirties and living in a country town has witnessed people experiencing unemployment and family breakdown drawn together because of a common desperate situation. 'They are finding resources within themselves to support each other in building a real basic caring community,' she said. 'God is behind that.' She is supported by a sister in her late fifties who believes that people are becoming aware of the existence of goodness through help given by others. A sixty-year-old sister would not miss her work with Meals on Wheels 'for all the tea in China'. Another sister in her late fifties admired the work done by the Kiwanis, a group of tradesmen who give their skills voluntarily and unobtrusively to help those in need. A fifty-two-year-old sister remarked: 'God is moving very much in the hearts of ordinary people.' She told the story of a thirty-five-year-old man dying from cancer and leaving a wife and five small children. Neighbours got together to buy a water-bed so his last weeks in his home would be as comfortable as possible. They rostered themselves to see to the garden and to help the wife in the house. 'Right around this country there is a lot of small support work going

135

on. There is a spirituality in that because they are supporting people not only physically and financially but also emotionally.' A seventy-year-old sister commented: 'You only have to listen to what people are talking about and what they are concerned with to realise they are becoming more actively caring.'

Several sisters spoke about 'the emerging age of the laity'. More and more lay people are attending theological lectures and theological colleges on a part-time or full-time basis. According to a sister in her late forties: 'The laity are surging ahead with a vision and a hope and a life of prayer: they have a vitality often lacking among religious.' She described some religious as 'navel-gazers. They keep on saying they are tired, thus justifying a slack existence. A lot of religious are just bored.' She hastened to add: 'I wouldn't want to generalise too much. There are religious women with their golden jubilees behind them branching out into one or two new ministries.'

Recalling Alexander Solzhenitsyn's Nobel Prize acceptance speech in which he said that Western society can regain its spiritual values only through art, a forty-seven-year-old sister pointed to the thousands of Australians who viewed the Impressionist Exhibition and the Monet Exhibition, the crowds who go to the opera and to the ballet. She sees in these attendances not only a witness to spiritual values inherent in people, but also a positive fostering of their spiritual values. Acknowledging that appreciation of art is fairly embryonic in Australia, she said: 'Through art you can see the flashes of God breaking in on Australian culture. That is what we as church should touch.' A sixty-year-old sister noted an Australian love of the good things of nature:

When I spend time watching people windsurfing and swimming in the sea, I can't help thinking that that part of our life must lead us to inward reflection on what life is all about. In the outback, too, people are riding horses or driving cars alone over long distances. That solitude in the bush must result in depthing for them.

A few sisters in their thirties support the view expressed by one of them that Australians are coming of age.

In letting go of England and America we are being forced to examine who we are as people. We are searching for our identity in such movies as *Breaker Morant, Gallipoli, Burke and Wills.* We are trying to grapple with our origins—a convict settlement— which has resulted in us seeing ourselves as second-rate people. Even the things we celebrate, Gallipoli and the Eureka Stockade, are our failures.

A sister in her mid-forties believes that 'We are beginning to stand up and be proud that we are Australians. We are beginning to become more aware of the good things we have going for us.'

Brothers

Of the brothers interviewed, 8 per cent were unable to speak positively on Australian society; 16 per cent spoke only of movements within the Catholic Church, and, after discussing church issues and with further prompting, another 16 per cent went on to include the non-church issues. The comments of the latter together with those of the remaining 60 per cent follow.

Brothers specifically commented on a growing awareness of and concern for those whom a brother in his late thirties called 'the broken people', the disadvantaged and the minorities. Five brothers mentioned the government's part in aiding financially the elderly and ill and in raising the interest of people in social issues. Huge budgets, said one, have been given for multicultural education. Three brothers mentioned the move to secure land rights for Aborigines as another example of help given to a minority. Some brothers see this concern as an extension of the traditional sense of mateship among Australians. Mateship lay behind generous responses to natural disasters: 'Bush fire appeals are always supported generously,' one brother said. 'There is the expectation you bog in and help.' Mateship was also seen in the growing awareness of the concept of the global village: Australians contribute generously to deprived people overseas.

Four brothers foresee an increasing interest in religion and spiritual values. One cited the example of non-Catholics attending the papal Mass on the Pope's last visit to Australia: their attendance proved to him their acknowledgement of the significance of a religious event. Another spoke about 'grass roots movements among a minority of people seeking spiritual values'. Religious rivalry, claimed a brother in his sixties, has almost disappeared from the Australian scene. Growing interest in peace and justice issues provided proof of Australians' development in maturity: the anti-war feeling in Australia, according to a brother in his thirties, is 'God-given'.

Christianity is developing, but not necessarily in the Catholic Church, reported a brother in his fifties; many of his ex-students have left the church but have become very good apostolic men. A brother in his forties has similar views:

A new spirituality is emerging and I see it expressed in the lives of my students. They do not measure religion by church attendance. They have a greater variety of images of God and of relationships possible with him. I think we have had to go through a period — and we are still going through it — of falling away from an attitude to religion that was a bit meaningless. Going to Mass on Sundays was more or less a support system for a lot of people who weren't thinking their way through spiritual values. What I call this new spirituality is relationship based: it puts the emphasis on the maintenance of a relationship that will lead people towards the right approach to God without needing to educate them in every do and don't. It is a spirituality with which Australians will come to identify, but they need to be reassured it is valid. People are frightened to come out and say it is not so important to attend Sunday Mass.

If one can make people feel comfortable about the way in which they live their faith, and if we offered opportunities to them to experience a variety of models of community, of spirituality and prayer life, then they would respond. From that response would develop new communities, more open and sensitive to one another. It would be a less institutionalised church, but it would be a much more warm and human place for people.

Priests

While 20 per cent of priests were unable to list any positive movement within Australian society that is helping people to become better human beings, 32 per cent immediately connected the question with the Catholic Church and spoke specifically of movements within it. The attitude underlying their comments coincided with that expressed by a priest in his forties: 'God's working in everything but on a fairly long-term basis.'

Several within the remaining 48 per cent of priests praised the supporters of the peace movement — some, they said, had no real knowledge of God, yet were in touch with something Christian and related to God. In this category they placed the conservationists, nuclear disarmament groups, animal-lovers and the various organisations trying to alleviate human suffering, the groups treating alcoholics, drug addicts, helping the poor and disadvantaged. A priest in his sixties placed such organisations under corporal works of mercy: 'Because they are works of mercy, they are a reflection of God's mercy, even though the people involved wouldn't see it like that.'

A priest in his thirties pointed out that trade unionists were struggling to establish justice among workers: 'They identify their work as merely human, but I see God's hand there.' Australians were also seen as being more aware of needs of people outside their country and giving generous aid to them. 'For the first time', said one priest, 'we are perhaps realising there is one God and we are all one people.' Two priests mentioned smaller self-help groups that emerge to help sections of people. A priest in his fifties said: 'People are reaching out from the depths of their own suffering to help others in like situations, for example, in the loss of a baby.'

According to a priest in his mid-thirties, the superficiality of Australian society is drawing more people to churches and churches are working more closely together in a desire for a shared vision. One priest said:

People are full of good will. Although they can't always express it, they are groping for spiritual values. They are becoming more aware of each other's humanity and treating it with more respect. They have a growing sense of responsibility for what happens in the world.

As another priest said: 'God is no longer a Catholic, nor does he belong to one race.' Not all, however, are turning to churches. In his professional work, a priest sees 'a dramatic search for spirituality', but the people he meets 'tell me they don't feel they fit within church structures. They find them too constricting, but they are genuine searchers after God and salvation.' The same priest has come into contact with people living in community and praying together. 'The real issue for them', he said, 'is relationship and community, a good basis on which to find God.'

Several priests emphasised that Australians were desiring better relationships with one another and one specifically mentioned the high expectations of married relationships. Even though these sometimes led to divorce courts, he recognises such high ideals as moral progress, and divorce facilities, although often abused, as protection of the rights of the injured. In his opinion, the fact that there are fewer unwanted children today was also a big step forward in social and personal morality. Divorce and birth control, he added, still posed a real problem for the Catholic Church: 'We have a gap between the pastoral and doctrinal approaches which isn't very fair for lay people.'

Negative changes

Sisters

Religious were also asked to comment on anything in Australian society that they believed was preventing people from developing as better human beings. Of sisters, 4 per cent made no comment and 4 per cent merely deplored the smaller church attendances. The majority of the remaining 92 per cent spoke briefly, mainly in clichés, about the evils of drugs, drink, child abuse, abortion, pornography and the permissive society in general. One thirty-nine-year-old sister, however, was more incisive:

> People rant and rave about drugs, crime and so on. I don't honestly know. I can't label all that anti-kingdom. I think that the forces that prevent us from reaching out to one another are the things that are anti-kingdom — the things that keep me centred on myself.

There was general agreement that selfishness lurked behind the evils of consumerism and materialism, the 'buy now, pay later' campaigns. 'People equate happiness with possessions rather than with the quality of their own life,' commented a sister in her fifties, 'and advertisements aimed at upper and middle classes reinforce this.' As a thirty-four-year-old sister remarked: 'Individuals are saying, "As long as I have my car, my big house, my television and my boat, I have my little kingdom. I don't need anyone."' She saw this aim to be independent of others as ultimately destructive for Australian society. Australians, according to a seventy-one-year-old sister, have to come to terms with the profit motive and acknowledge that all human beings have a right to human dignity and human subsistence.

A few sisters noted that individual millionaires are gradually taking control of more business concerns with 'the little man' being squeezed out of the economy. The increasing size of bureaucracy was also seen as bad for Australians: greed for power and money extend throughout society, including the Government. A forty-two-year-old sister believed that parliamentarians are more interested in squabbling for power among themselves than in ruling the country. 'In New South Wales', said a thirty-nine-year-old sister, 'the whole system of law and government seems to be riddled with corruption.' A sister in her late fifties stated:

> I go to many meetings connected with local government, and there is a lot of corruption among officials supposedly working for the good of the country. They work the system to get more money, and the people who are supposed to benefit receive nothing.

Two sisters commented on the selfish militancy of trade unions, but another looked at the other side of the coin:

> We Australians have only short-term thinking. For example, if Joh [Sir Joh Bjelke-Petersen, then Premier of Queensland] is able to beat a union and that makes life more comfortable for me, I settle into comfortable apathy about it and hope all unions will be knocked into place. My short-term needs are met, and I don't think of what will happen to my freedom in the long term.

141

Unemployment was mentioned by a few sisters. It was seen as taking away the dignity of young people. 'I feel', confessed one forty-four-year-old sister, 'there is a hopelessness resulting from not having a job, and it pains me.' Working with young people as she does, a forty-year-old sister recognises among them a worship of individualism difficult to counter:

There is a whole cult of youth, of glamorising youth. Simultaneously, the stages in the proper maturing of the whole person is ignored. There is an adoration of youth and their physical beauty, which can work against the whole understanding of the spiritual dimension of life.

Secularism, according to a few sisters, is rampant in Australia. A fifty-one-year-old sister summarised their comments:

Australian culture is very secular, and I think I am tainted with it—a lot of religious may be. We have a narrow concept of religion; we have an inferiority complex about it. I am just climbing out of that. There is repressed self-image and repressed spiritual dimension in Australian culture.

Only one sister, forty-nine years old, commented on the attitude to sports. She sees it as totally male-oriented in Australia; football, basketball and racing draw huge crowds. These are the sports with heavy emphasis on winning and money, all to do with the man's world:

The Australian culture is deeply, basically ockerish and afraid of the feminine, the realm of being. To its detriment, Australian society downgrades woman, and qualities of tenderness and gentleness are not valued.

Several sisters noted that the Australian attitude to authority is ambivalent, with its origin in our convict days. As one sixty-three-year-old sister remarked: 'We put people on pedestals and then knock them off.' A younger sister had this to say:

I was once proud of the anti-authoritarian stance in Australia. But the unquestioning nature of it makes me wonder now. There's been an anti-authoritarianism which was the Ned Kelly kind with a romantic flavour. Now there seems to be a movement to the right: 'Let's get everybody straightened out because there's too much violence.' We didn't know why we were anti-authority, and we don't know why we're suddenly becoming more authoritarian. There's a lack of a reflective nature in a lot of Australians.

Brothers

Brothers listed the obvious factors operating against a consciousness of spiritual and human values: over-dependence on drugs, alcohol and tranquillisers, pornographic videos, sex and violence in television series and materialism in society. Television portrays to youngsters a world they evaluate as real, making them blind to the purpose and value of life itself. Five brothers specifically criticised the media in general. One saw a movement in the media that appears to be deliberately breaking down the sense of morality and values. A brother in his thirties supported his view: 'The media encourages permissiveness and too much tolerance for homosexuality.'

Several brothers assert that false values are dominating Australian lives. A brother pointed out that young couples expect a new brick home, with all its modern comforts, and two cars, with the result that these material expectations dictate the nature of their relationship, the number and time of arrival of children, and the amount of care and concern they have for others. He believes that both state and Catholic schools have cultivated these values and wants church leaders to speak out clearly against such a frantic search for personal wealth and comfort. Competitiveness in industry also encourages selfishness. A brother in his fifties said: 'You have to beat the other guy as long as it is within the law. People look for loopholes in laws, not for the spirit of them. We have lost sight of community goals in our strong push to get what we want.' A thirty-year-old brother commented on another worrying aspect in society: 'More people are escaping from problems. They are unwilling to commit themselves, with the result we have a lot of thirty-year-old teenagers around.'

Of the brothers interviewed, 32 per cent spoke directly on religion. One deplored the Australian indifference to organised religion: 'Religion is irrelevant to many people and we should be addressing the religious issue as strongly as we do the unemployment.' Another brother put forward his opinion: 'We have gone past the stage where we pigeonhole God. The religious practice of Australians is more a civic thing than a personal worship of a God. It is tied up with Anzac Day, funerals and marriages.'

Several brothers spoke about the emergence of what they termed the New Right. A brother in his forties sees the New Right wanting to turn back the social consciousness of Australians and said: 'There can be no divorce between life and worship. Too many emphasise Mass on Sundays as essential, then live the rest of the week as if religion did not exist.' Another spelt out the situation more clearly:

> The movement that goes under the name of the New Right is dangerous, as it hides behind a veneer of respectability that seems to be in line with the traditional church, and often it is churchgoing people who espouse these values. Just witness the hot debate that goes on over the statements of the Commission for Justice and Peace. As soon as someone asks for justice for some groups, he is automatically branded either a communist or a communist sympathiser.
>
> Some people who are public figures in church and in politics espouse values that have little to do with the Gospel but a lot to do with conservative politics. Not that all conservative politics are wrong, but some would still opt for a White Australia policy. A lot of people would say that religious and clergy should not make statements of a 'political' nature. What that normally means is 'Don't criticise the system', even when it's often inherently unjust. The church in Africa, Asia and South America is pointing the way and saying: 'To be authentically Christian in today's world is to bring injustices to the notice of the world.'

A brother in his forties commented on what he saw as the basic problem in Australian society:

There is a real gap, a split in the lives of people. I see it in the members of my own family. There are the effects of something missing right through the Australian culture. Otherwise, why the unmitigated hedonism, the desperate scramble for elusive happiness in the pursuit of the almighty dollar? Traditional Christianity, including Australian Catholicism, is irrelevant to the Australian scene. No, I should say Catholicism as we have it in Australia is irrelevant, because it's a mixture of cultures and Irish Catholicism grafted onto our land. It just doesn't work. We have to develop a truly Australian church for Australians.

Priests

Drugs, alcohol, pornography, materialism, corruption in political and judicial areas were all mentioned by priests as factors preventing people from maturing into better human beings. One young priest in his twenties believes that a great evil in society today is the feminist movement:

It's feminism gone mad. There are definite roles for male and female . . . the man to be the breadwinner in the family and the woman to be the mother. Women have some grudge against a male-dominated world, and I don't see that as a good thing.

A priest in his sixties was concerned about family life from another angle:

There is an enormous amount of legalism in Australia, and a lot of people suffer because of our laws. Many laws don't favour real human values. Laws regulating taxation, for example, are punishing the young family groups.

Several priests commented about the selfishness of Australians. One older man said: 'A good recession would help people by making them do with less and appreciate what they've got.'

The majority of priests were most concerned about the diminution of values intrinsic to human nature. 'The true evil in the world', said a priest in his twenties, 'is the loss of the sense of one's own self-worth and Australians are losing their

sense of feeling worthwhile.' Several priests agreed with one
in his thirties who said:

> The type of dependency created by the welfare system is
> destructive. Unemployment eventually destroys young people's
> self-respect, respect for others and their own identity. When that
> happens it is difficult for them to hear God speak.

Moreover, as another priest pointed out, the media and
advertisements deepen this poverty of spirit:

> People's minds are being controlled, and emotional responses are
> conditioned. They have robot-like reactions. Australians have
> certain attitudes—some are racial, others to do with sex stereo-
> types, some with social status. For example, if you have a job,
> you're OK. If you haven't, you're a bum.

A priest in his fifties remarked: 'We have a consumerism
mentality, with the result people are made to feel more or less
dignified on the basis of what possessions they have or
haven't.' A second priest in his fifties, however, has recently
abandoned his belief that consumerism as a way of life
should be attacked:

> Consumerism is built into the economy of our country and is so
> much part of our lives that I don't see any point in preaching
> against it. We must try to come to terms with consumerism,
> Christianise it, which I don't know how to do.

Australians, according to a priest in his early seventies,
have had too much of a good life: 'If they can't get what they
want legitimately, some are even prepared to seize it with
violence.' Hence people are living in fear, locking themselves
in at night. A priest in his early thirties said:

> There is much loneliness in Australian society and, what is
> worse, anonymity. People can live next door to neighbours for
> fifteen years and not know their names. To many people, then,
> life is losing its meaning. When life loses its meaning, it loses it
> value.

As governments extend control, personal rights are being whittled away. A priest in his late thirties commented: 'People in the street feel they haven't the opportunity to make any decisions about their lives. Institutions are taking over, and people are becoming lethargic about their rights.'

Against such a background, where he sees the moral fibre of people is being sapped, a fifty-six-year-old priest said:

> Australians are searching for the good life and money. You don't need God or spiritual values if you've got or are looking for these things, so religion is irrelevant. Australians aren't anti-God or anti-religion — God and religion are just not wanted. I don't know how you can convince people that they need something more than material things.

Struggling with change

Sisters

I asked religious men and women if they felt it appropriate for themselves as religious to take an active part in affirming the importance of spiritual values and creating a more positive environment for Australians. Interested as they are in important issues, sisters feel hesitant about publicly asserting their views either verbally or with their presence, for this has not been in the tradition of sisters within Australia. When a seventy-three-year-old sister told me it was more appropriate for sisters to pray rather than to take action, she was identifying with past expectations of sisters. So was a sixty-year-old when she said she was uncertain whether it was appropriate for sisters to support or denounce movements: 'The peace movement, for example, seems to have a communistic background. A priest told me not to become involved, to leave it awhile to see which way it will go.'

Anxious to support what they acknowledge are worthwhile movements, yet uncertain as to the best way to do this, sisters appear willing to follow strong leadership in this area. A fifty-nine-year-old sister said:

147

I'm very interested in women's issues. I'm not active in them or well informed about them, but I would be prepared to give support to those taking steps to improve women's situation. But I need someone to take the initiative and to stimulate me.

Sisters are recognising that they have to assume responsibility for public issues. A thirty-nine-year-old sister confessed:

I'm in two minds over the whole nuclear disarmament issue and I should study it more—I'm too busy doing the urgent thing instead of the important. I am doing nothing to help the children in my school to cope with a nuclear future. I'd like to do so.

A fifty-year-old sister commented:

At this point I am not ready to go public with my opinions. But I believe that is what is being asked of us as religious, and some big decisions may follow such action by sisters. It may even mean change in the relationship with the hierarchy of the church.

Admitting that she is not yet courageous enough 'to stand up and be counted', a thirty-seven-year-old was definite that she 'would like society to know how a group of religious women stood on certain issues'. She offered a reason for what she saw as a lack of commitment:

A lot of us are still struggling with the new image of religious life, and, until that settles a little bit, it is difficult for us to speak out, because we are still grappling with who we are and where we want to stand on certain issues.

Another sister in her thirties pointed out a second reason:

We have moved into the mainstream of culture so much that we aren't really signs of anything very much to people at the moment, except that we are part of the middle class establishment of the whole power structures that exist. I think we are called to move back to where we are meant to be, and where we once were, that is, on the margins. The margins have changed. They are not those of the past.

A forty-year-old sister recalled that some sisters joined the unionists in their protest against the Queensland Government's stand on the electricians' strike: 'There are two sides to every question, and perhaps they were only seeing one side. When we do protest and speak out, we have to be sure that we are being just to both sides.' This sense of justice is strong among some sisters and would evidently determine their mode of support. As a forty-four-year-old sister reasoned:

We can stand too strongly with anti-abortion and anti-nuclear groups, and as a result the community at large would see us as unapproachable and rigid in our thinking. I do not see it advisable to be very obviously demonstrative on debatable matters.

A sister in her early sixties supported her: 'We can't rush in fanatically. We'd do more harm than good.'

Some sisters are already actively engaged in raising people's awareness of important issues. A forty-year-old sister involves her primary school class with a group of elderly, so that they will be more sympathetic towards the aged. A few sisters in their seventies run prayer groups in their parishes. Others see themselves as leaven: one works with a group in a poor suburb, stimulating their initiative and encouraging them to agitate for services they need in the community. Two others deliberately give their opinion on important issues to the groups with whom they work and encourage people to take action when possible. 'I write letters to the right people on anything about which I am unhappy,' said a sister in her forties,' and I urge others to do so.' A number of sisters regularly use letter-writing as their instrument for good. A sister in her late forties is working specifically to encourage and empower women to live as creatively as they can: 'I have found that when women have built up their spirituality and freedom, their husbands also change and appreciate the difference in their wives.'

Another sister, in her mid-fifties, is involved with the work of the Salvation Army. One in her early forties encourages and supports people who have to go to the Housing Commission or the Social Services, as she recognises the need for such encouragement: 'Disadvantaged people have little education and little power over their own lives. They are frightened to make waves in case they lose the little they have.' A sister in her mid-forties speaks out publicly and regularly on important issues: 'I know quite well that in speaking out I'm going to make enemies.' Others take part in peace marches and in some protest marches. They are not indiscriminate supporters. As one said: 'I first think about it very seriously as I am not a natural protestor.'

On the whole, sisters more readily support what they identify as positive issues: they are wary of speaking against issues. As a sister in her late thirties remarked: 'I am not sure that, by speaking against evil, you can do anything productive. By becoming involved you can contribute to a hopelessness and became part of a whole manipulative process.' A fifty-two-year-old sister agreed with her: 'We have only a certain amount of emotional energy, so we should support the positive movements rather than spread ourselves too thinly in counteracting negative movements.'

Not only does a thirty-one-year-old sister show solidarity with those making positive options, she also tries to remain in sympathetic touch with those who aren't: 'You give up hope if you ostracise people.' There is, therefore, clear evidence that sisters will become more visible in public concerns. As a thirty-five-year-old sister said: 'We've got to move. We can't afford to sit back too much longer. We religious have to become more interested in issues outside our work.' And a sixty-three-year-old sister was optimistic: 'Very definitely individuals are moving. It will be individuals who finally convince their congregations that they need to take an active stance in many areas.'

Brothers

Eleven brothers support the public involvement of religious in issues affecting the welfare of Australians; of these, two are actively participating, one taking part in demonstration marches, the other working with local councils to improve conditions for the disadvantaged. These brothers emphasised that before religious become actively involved they must have necessary information and skills so that their presence as religious would not be exploited. Two brothers were emphatic that the role of religious was not in the public forum. The remaining brothers stressed that much good can be done within one's own area of influence. A young brother said: 'What I stand for must be a witness for good. In trying to be a secure, stable person I am providing something for kids that hopefully counterbalances the lack in many of their lives.' Giving affirmation and encouragement to the people among whom they work is seen as a positive contribution to Australian society: 'The school', said a brother in his forties, 'can be built up as a community of faith whereby people there are supported in their values.'

Priests

When asked how religious could help Australian society, the majority of priests agreed with one in his mid-forties who said: 'All we can do as religious is to live out our charism and be a sign for those who have eyes to see.' Five priests disagreed. One in his late forties spoke for them when he said: 'We should be in the market place for our voices to be heard. We should be right in the thick of it in a way which is not now officially approved in the church. Working in politics would be a good way to help change things.'

A priest in his late fifties accounted for what he saw as the lack of influence religious have had on Australian people:

Religious in Australia have not been educated in social or academic affairs. For too long we've been in a sub-culture with the emphasis on being obedient and not thinking for ourselves and even of being a little anti-intellectual. We've been afraid of getting mixed up with the world and losing our vocation. We've protected our lives from society and failed to update our social ideas.

The overall impression was that most priests concentrated on their Catholic flock and felt fairly helpless—as did most brothers and sisters—in face of an Australian society to whom religion is irrelevant and ignored.

Conclusion

A relatively large percentage of religious men and women immediately identified Australian society with the Catholic Church—a regrettable, yet understandable identification since, until recent times, so many (especially brothers and sisters) moved only in Catholic circles and worked in Catholic schools and hospitals. Society's main problems today appear outside the ken of most religious. When, for example, the religious interviewed mentioned such problems as drugs, few manifested a deep concern or sympathy for those addicted. Fewer still assumed any responsibility for living in a society that has allowed such problems to develop. It was almost as if the majority were behind invisible, antiseptic walls.

I gained a very strong impression that most interviewees regarded Catholics as a separate, not fully assimilated group within the whole Australian society. There is, however, a small minority of religious, mainly women, who are today working outside church organisations or parishes. These, together with another small minority working within the church framework, have widened their concept of religion and are becoming more civic minded. Their ecumenical attitudes are strengthening and they are not so closely identifying themselves with 'Catholic' thinking. They are beginning to recognise their responsibilities as Australian citizens. If congregations as groups encourage and act on that recognition, they will make a strong impact on what one sister has described as 'the repressed spiritual dimension in Australian culture'. As a sixty-year-old sister remarked: 'Ten thousand dedicated religious women should have more impact than they do today on Australian society and its values.'

Religious men and women and the Catholic Church

8

Religious and laity

*F*or centuries religious men and women have been undeniably a recognised integral and important part of the Catholic Church: they are usually acknowledged as its professional arm. After Vatican II, however, came the laity's realisation of their own importance in the church, followed by changes in the lifestyle of religious, especially of women religious. Both of these changes led to shifts in attitudes regarding the status and role of religious men and women in the church. Not only did the laity re-evaluate their status and role, but the religious themselves re-assessed them, and again, because external changes were more dramatically obvious within women's congregations, both laity and religious re-evaluated more critically the role of religious women in the church.

I asked interviewees how they perceived the laity's attitude towards them. It became obvious that because religious men and women today have differing lifestyles and values, they experience a variety of reactions from the laity. Older people's reactions tend to rely on former traditions: religious are on pedestals, and they can cause scandal by being too friendly or by wearing casual clothes. There are a few religious influenced by such expectations. A brother in his fifties, for example, always wears the traditional black clothes and white collar outside the monastery: 'I'd prefer not to, but I know from their comments people are pleased to see me dressed as a religious brother.' Many religious agreed with a priest in his forties: 'Laity can be too deferential. because they feel religious are doing something extraordinary, know a lot about prayer and have the answers to life's problems.'

This is not always the case, however, as another priest pointed out: 'Educated people are critically evaluative, tend to dismiss religious still operating in the traditional mould, but enjoy working with religious who share their view of the Gospels.'

Laity—and sisters—feel a certain ambiguity about the identity and place of religious women within the church and within society. A fifty-two-year-old sister said:

People with whom we relate are a little confused about who we are and what we are doing—as perhaps we are. They are a little bit fearful that changes in religious life will demand from them more involvement in the work of the church. People can find it frightening to contend with us as individual human beings.

Sometimes there is a reluctance on the part of the laity to respond to sisters as women, and there can be an expectation of certain actions and responses, simply because they are religious. A forty-four-year-old sister said that laity can be surprised if a sister says 'Damn' or takes a day off to go to the Blue Mountains. Another sister in her mid-thirties is often amused by people's reactions to her:

> People can be talking about a de facto relationship or something like that, then half-way through the conversation they realise who you are and immediately begin apologising profusely for their topic of conversation and for the language they used. They have no idea of how close a sister comes to the nitty-gritty of life.

Several sisters noted that when people know them well they are very accepting of the changes within religious life and happier that sisters are more approachable.

Probably because of the greater visibility of brothers in schools, the laity appear more certain of their relevance. 'In my area', said a brother in his forties, 'we are still the kings in grass castles.' A brother in his thirties remarked: 'The religious brother is very much accepted because he is a brother, no matter what sort of a person he is.' Another brother in his thirties had a reservation: 'Although most Catholics depend on you as on a rock foundation and permanent help in problems, others see you as a Clayton's job—the religious you have when you're not having a religious.' More than sisters, brothers hold that to be a religious means assuming spiritual responsibilities: 'I expect to be seen as serious about preaching the kingdom in the way I live my life,' said one brother.

Priests are more confident of their place in the church and of respect from the laity. A number, however, commented that young people do not see religious men and women as relevant.

A young priest was with a number of young people when they were wondering what they would do in life: 'I said to one that maybe God wanted him to be a religious, and they all laughed spontaneously in a way that showed me they thought that was a stupid suggestion.'

The morale of many religious men and women, especially the latter, are affected by their realisation that a section of the laity consider them irrelevant and out of the mainstream of life. One result is that some congregations have become involved in programmes aimed at revitalising their members and, consequently, their ministry.

When religious men and women were asked if they perceived any difference between themselves and the laity, they spontaneously accepted the reality of a difference that, they confessed, was very difficult to define. Only a few elderly sisters saw the difference in a directly spiritual way. A seventy-year-old sister said: 'I am a spouse of Christ, so there is a difference. In all honesty, religious life is a higher mode of existence, and more is expected of us by God and by the people.' Not all elderly sisters agree. One in her mid-seventies questioned the values operating in her life and wondered if the difference did not weigh in favour of the laity:

> I stayed with my blood sister for a couple of weeks. I tried to make time for my prayers and Mass. She, however, was thinking of what she could do to help a poor, old, diabetic man and how she could help this son-in-law and that daughter. She was always thinking of what she could do to better the lives of others. I was ashamed that she was so much more thoughtful and kind than I.

Five priests, but no brother, recognised a spiritual difference between themselves and the laity. After all, commented a sixty-five-year-old priest,

> Religious by their vows commit themselves to a more intense striving for perfection than do laity. Religious are also a sign of what striving for perfection ought to be, and priests are set apart to share with Christ a mediator's role between God and his people.

The great majority of religious men and women see the

difference between themselves and the laity in their lifestyle and what this enables them to do. Where lay people commit themselves to their family, the religious, having publicly taken the vows of chastity, poverty and obedience and committed themselves to life in community, are ideally able to focus on Christ and service. Most religious seemed to agree with the statement of a priest in his mid-thirties:

> Fundamentally, there is no difference. We are all called to the same Gospel values, even though I'm obviously choosing to live out my baptismal commitment by a way of life different from the laity.

Most religious admit that they in religious life have been given so many more opportunities to know and love God than their lay friends, and for that they are grateful and acknowledge that they have not profited as they might have done from such opportunities. A brother in his forties said: 'Such opportunities impose a responsibility on religious to reflect on life and to give the benefits of that reflection to others caught up in the hurly burly of activities.'

Today religious are more willing to accept and act upon this responsibility. More knowledgeable about and more sympathetically involved in lives and problems of lay people than ever before, they are questioning some moral rulings of the institutional church, especially in the areas of sexual morality, that have caused tension and perplexity to very many of the laity. When asked if they thought the Australian Catholic Church would change its attitudes in moral matters, all except nine sisters, one brother and three priests spoke solely in terms of sexual morality. The small minority would like to see the social teaching of the church carefully examined and support the statement of the brother: 'We have an enormous way to go as a church to wake up to the demands of the Gospel. There is a large gap between the first and third worlds, and the Catholic Church is closely identified with the first world. It is still too tied up in secular values.' And a priest in his mid-thirties said: 'The hierarchy and people think capitalism is a sacred cow, and if you touch it you're automatically a communist.'

Of the religious interviewed, 87 per cent of sisters, 36 per cent of brothers and 80 per cent of priests hope that the Catholic Church will alter its attitude in some areas of sexual morality. Explicitly or implicitly, they support the statement of a priest in his late twenties: 'Basically what is right must be so for all time, but ways of expressing morality change, the application of principles in individual cases will be different.'

While upholding the church's principles in sexual morality, the majority of religious assert strongly that the church should interpret more compassionately and understandingly those principles. A brother in his forties spoke for them when he said:

It's not the principles of the church's teachings on sexual morality that should change—they're sound—but the way in which they're sometimes taught. It has invariably been presented as an all-or-nothing situation, sexual sins being always mortal. We have a long way to go before we can present authentically Catholic teaching on sexual morality.

According to a brother in his fifties, the Australian Catholic Church is still too governed by conservative Irish and Polish mentality. The result, he pointed out, is obvious: 'We are presented with laws that are basically ideals, not true laws. A black-and-white situation is usually presented. People are now realising that their lives can't be regulated by a textbook's list.'

Religious on the whole are very sympathetic towards people in unsuccessful marriages. Most sisters judge it advisable to speed the process of annulments and to eliminate its hurtful aspects. They believe the church should not exclude divorced couples from its full membership, and some religious would accept a second marriage. 'I do not believe', said a sister in her thirties, 'people have to experience a life of loneliness and feelings of failure because a marriage did not work.' As a brother in his forties commented:

The church should certainly present the ideal for marriage, but if one does fail, then it can only be harmful to the family to maintain it. With no other statement in the Gospels does the church take such a literal stand. . . . People riddled with prejudice receive holy communion, so I have no hesitation in telling divorced people to go too. It's absolute humbug to say that that group of people can't receive communion. After all, the Lord did say, 'Come to me all you who labour.'

Most religious recognise that change is a natural part of the church's development and agree with a sixty-year-old priest who defined the core of the issue:

It depends on what you understand the church to be. There's not much change in the hierarchical institution, but if you are talking about the people of God, yes, I see vast changes. Catholic laity reflect their own society, and in some issues they reach a stage where they make up their own minds. The hierarchical church dithered for years about the contraceptive pill, so the laity just had to make up their own minds.

Another priest pointed out a result of people thinking for themselves: 'Today one can dissent and still belong to the Catholic Church regardless of the official view: people go to the sacraments where a generation ago they would have removed themselves as being out of line with church teaching.'

A brother in his early thirties also sees the clergy's power waning as laity become more spiritually adult. His view of the Catholic Church is that of several religious, and one brother in his forties outlined it:

If the church is the people of God and the hierarchical system, then somewhere along the line we need to put credence in the infallibility of the faithful. People do bring about changes. The hierarchical church can exhort and forbid, but if the people think and do otherwise, the hierarchical church quietens down. The pill, for example, is a bit of a dead issue now.

According to a thirty-nine-year-old sister, the Catholic principle of the supremacy of conscience is not clearly emphasised, because the role of the priest is continually protected and because the church does not believe an individual is capable of making his or her own decisions. As a forty-four-year-old sister remarked: 'We have to educate people to understand they have a right to make an informed decision for themselves.' A forty-nine-year-old sister said:

> The people did not know the primary principle of choosing the lesser of two evils. Had they known, the choice between family tension and privation and taking the pill would have been easier and less guilt-ridden. . . The Catholic Church has a rich tradition of moral scholarship, but it is only one voice among many traditions. It must realise that its members will listen carefully to all voices, including that of the church before, as human beings responsible before God, making decisions sometimes about life and death.

One priest commented on a greater awareness of the ideals of the Gospel as opposed to black-and-white commandments: 'The law doesn't apply in the same way to all people at any one time.' Besides, as a thirty-six-year-old priest said: 'More people now realise their own responsibility and individual gifts, and they're not going to hand these over to a heavy authority because they know it is wrong to do that.'

A few priests are passing on their thinking. One in his early sixties said:

> I think morality is a personal matter. I listen carefully to what the institutional church has to say, but I wouldn't have any hesitation in going against it if I believed I was right. I don't advise people to do this but I support them if they do.

The institutional church

Sisters

Religious men and women have ambiguous reactions to the institutional church. When asked if she saw the Australian Catholic Church as an institution effectively bringing Christ's presence to people today, a seventy-eight-year-old sister voiced what all but three sisters faced with the same question seemed to feel: 'I am uneasy about this question.' Their unease arose from a feeling that any public criticism of the Australian Catholic Church savoured of disloyalty to it and undermined their own identity because laity and some religious themselves identify religious men and women with the institutional church. Loyalty to the Catholic Church and a strongly rooted adherence to its ideals struggled with a desire to take an opportunity to voice anonymously their honest feelings and thoughts about the present position of the church as they have experienced it. A thirty-nine-year-old sister summed up the general reaction:

> I have always had a great love for the church, and I have some difficulty in rejecting it in any way and saying it has a bad image. If I rejected it, I would be denying part of who I am. I believe that the institutional church cannot be separated from the church Christ called together. But I think the institution is due for an overhaul. I would like to see the church presenting itself as a people called by Jesus to be a compassionate, caring community, interested in the truth of dogma and in the truth of people. The truth in the human heart is as important as the truth in the distilled wisdom of the church's experience.

Sisters defined the institution of the church as consisting of bishops and clergy. Several sisters, including one aged twenty-five, believed that the majority of Australians view institutional churches negatively and cynically. A forty-two-year-old sister said: 'As an institution, the Catholic Church does not understand where people are at, culturally and spiritually. It does not understand the needs of those it professes to serve.' A sister in her thirties saw the same results from another angle:

> The Catholic Church as an institution is very caught up with other institutions in society. It is what I call a power bloc and its main focus is maintaining itself, the institutional church. Because so many middle class align themselves with it, the church is a million miles away from little people desperately in need of salvation, the message of the Gospel and a sense of hope in their lives. Most of us are so caught up in the institutional church we have no idea how to meet these people and the whole evangelical thing is not operating.

'As an institution,' said a fifty-six-year-old sister, 'the Australian Catholic Church sends shivers down my spine.'

Many sisters like to see church leaders not only taking a public stand on matters other than those related to sex and government funding for Catholic schools, but also taking positive action in social issues. As a forty-seven-year-old sister commented: 'The official Church is sadly absent from a lot of places where it should be.' 'There are so many things going on in Australian society,' said a forty-one-year-old sister, 'and our leaders are silent. The church remains in the age of steam, sandstone and incense.' A forty-three-year-old sister believes that the church may be trying to remain neutral in public issues, but its silence means it is accepting the status quo. A thirty-six-year-old sister wondered what the church had done for oppressed people: 'Our leaders are fence-sitters. They sit and watch, and, mind you, so do religious.' A sister in her mid-fifties said:

> The institutional church doesn't have much influence because it preaches one thing and practises something else. If the church speaks out for social justice and equality, people see women within it prevented from more fully participating in the church's mission. They see a total contradiction.

Sisters acknowledged that the Catholic Church's effectiveness varied from diocese to diocese, from parish to parish. Secular clergy[1] dominate the church and most are traditional and legalistic in outlook. As a ninety-year-old sister remarked: 'We are in the old celtic system where the priest runs everything.' Many sisters believe that secular clergy as a group today have lost confidence in themselves and feel very threatened. Unwilling to adapt to Vatican II changes, some will not permit lay involvement because they are frightened of losing the power structures of a generation ago. In the eyes of some sisters they are victims of old traditions. A forty-nine-year-old sister gave her opinion:

---

1. Ordained priests who are subject and accountable to a diocesan bishop, but who do not take the vows of poverty and obedience. They do not belong to a religious order or congregation.

The secular priests have been taught to be administrators, not pastors. I have grown from feeling extremely angry with them to being sorry for them, because they are the most depleted of human beings. They have an almost impossible lifestyle, they get no feedback, and they live in isolation.

The clergy rule the church through a parish structure too big, too impersonal and other-worldly, where the emphasis is on worshipping God at Mass. 'It is tied down with the baggage of years,' exclaimed a sister in her forties. 'We are so caught up in our past structures and strategies that we are missing a lot of people.' A sixty-year-old sister explained:

> Most parishes have a core of workers who, under the supervision of the priest, run the show for those who go to Mass. The parish is not concerned with the vast bulk of the community who do not go to Mass and for whom the church is irrelevant.

The Catholic Church, according to a sixty-four-year-old sister, is not adapting quickly enough to the different groups within it, especially to the young people: 'There's not enough opportunity for youth to be involved in a way meaningful for them. There's not enough flexibility. Maybe it's just taken for granted that what is good for you is good for me.' The result, said a fifty-nine-year-old sister, is that 'the image of the well-established church in a suburb is one of dying and rigidity, one lacking joy and love'.

A sixty-three-year-old sister is one of many who do not envisage change coming from the top:

> It is a tremendous pity that in the Australian Catholic Church there is so much conservatism and so much fear at the top. When young priests, idealistic and ambitious to do good, become part of the hierarchy, they change. Fear seems to set in, a fear that they might make mistakes and perhaps lead people in the wrong direction. So, little is actually done.

A forty-eight-year-old sister said: 'A lot of our leaders are too distant from the people. They make demands on people's lives without being aware of or caring for the difficulties in their situation.' Doubts usually surfaced when sisters came into close contact with people who, because of their circumstances, judged they could not follow some of the church's dictates. This was the case for a sixty-year-old sister:

When I first began welfare work seven years ago, a lot of my ideas were challenged. The church says contraception is not on, but I was going to women's refuges and seeing women who had been battered and raped frequently by their husbands and I heard their side of the story. I met really good Catholic women denied the sacraments because they practised birth control just to be able to keep their family going: they literally couldn't cope with more children.

Bishops issued a beautiful article on the importance of migrants, but I was living in a parish where 80 per cent of the people were migrants and the parish didn't even know they existed. So there were a few things in the teachings of the church that didn't add up for me. When I talked my thoughts over with a priest, he told me that if my views continued to be so divergent from those of the church, I should not wear a religious habit. I was furious.

According to a sister in her forties:

Without realising it, the hierarchy is very much divorced from the people. They simply do not value the contribution of the laity. Five years ago, for example, the hierarchy seconded people for a committee and, as far as I know, they have not used one iota of anything done by the committee over that time.

Sisters willingly acknowledge that a few priests are successfully reshaping attitudes within the existing framework of parishes and are actively encouraging lay people to participate in liturgy and the affairs of the parish as far as possible within limits established by the hierarchy. A forty-three-year-old sister described one parish where the priest has established a true community: 'The presbytery is open house. The people know they are welcome to do something in the parish.' Within such effective pockets there is, as a forty-two-year-old sister said, more emphasis on caring for people: 'Individuals matter.' In country towns, isolated from cities, 'the face of the church is more likely to be a face of people not of the institution,' said a thirty-five-year-old sister working in such a town.

An Irish sister in her thirties was not the only one to observe that, even in such parishes, the priest is still seen as the power figure, the only one with authority: 'The laity can't take their rightful place within the parish until the priest gives the OK. He is still the only instrument to bring about growth.' And where he does not, a fifty-year-old sister lamented: 'The local church will die out with the older people. It should be a matter, not of inviting the laity to assume their responsibilities, but of the laity refusing to be deprived of them.' A sister in her thirties offered one factor determining lay passivity:

> The majority of our lay people are educated with a Catholic primary school understanding of justice and the priest's role, so they are ineffective in determining decisions within the parish. They can't do anything in face of Father's disapproval.

Referring to sisters, a forty-seven-year-old sister said:

> We do not have the freedom to move as ministers in any sense within the Australian Catholic Church. We, too, are dependent on a friendly parish priest before we can exercise the gifts we have for the people. We are all dependent on the priest in an extraordinary way.

The majority of sisters patiently accept the present situation within the church because they believe the church is slowly improving. A forty-two-year-old sister asked: 'What could be done without the institutional church? We can be very active and effective within it.' A sixty--year-old sister is confident: 'We as Catholics have to abide by the decision of the clergy and good will come from our obedience to them.' There are no doubts for a seventy-six-year-old sister: 'The Catholic Church is absolutely relevant to Australian society. A lot of things can go wrong, but God is there all the time.' Others appear a little less definite. 'Expectations can be too high,' explained a fifty-two-year-old sister. 'We have to remember the church is human.'

It is against a background of deep love for the Catholic Church that sisters offered positive suggestions whereby, in their belief and from their experience, the church might become more effective. They want bishops to become more involved as visible pastors, to invite true participation of relevant lay people and religious representatives in their annual conferences, to remove a parish priest's lifelong lease on his position and to exercise rightful and effective jurisdiction over incompetent parish priests. They want bishops to encourage priests to attend renewal programmes and to support them financially where necessary. (In at least one diocese a congregation of sisters not only financially supports several priests, but they also arrange for substitutes in the priests' parishes while they undertake renewal programmes.) They want lay people to take an active, responsible position in a parish organised by a truly representative parish council with genuine powers of decision-making. They want the interpretation of 'parish' to include non-churchgoers. A school principal said earnestly:

> We have to get out of that education-equals-the-church cycle and begin to put more energy, planning and personnel into evangelisation and education outside of schooling. A liturgy more alive than the 'four hymn' Mass is also needed.

Only four sisters mentioned they would like women to be ordained; many more are prepared to accept married clergy. Above all, sisters emphasised that a judgemental attitude must change to one of compassion, so that positive action will be taken to assist the disadvantaged, the needy and the sorrowful. Two sisters suggested that to ensure this would be done, parishes should be divided into smaller groups. Another suggestion was for two or three priests to live in community and operate in several parishes from the one centre.

Sisters hope that changes will come from the laity. An incident related by a sister reflected how bishop and priests in one diocese see themselves as an élite group and how the laity can sometimes be courageous enough to challenge this assumption: 'The celebration of an ordination was planned for the priests alone, until by constant niggling the parish council was given permission to organise a celebration to include lay people.' Another sister said:

For too long the laity have felt inadequate and hesitate even to share their faith with someone. They shy away from undertaking any responsibility in the church because they have always relied on the professionals, the priests and religious. There is some change now. Lay teachers in Catholic schools and the increasing number of men and women who study theology and the scriptures have far more confidence than their counterparts even of five years ago. They are more aware of what they can do and are anxious to do it.

Among the better-educated sisters, a vocal minority was struggling to preserve their integrity and to work in an increasingly difficult situation within a Catholic Church they feel has become divorced from the reality of life today. They commented on what one judged as 'almost a rejection of women, certainly their subjugation by the church'. A fifty-seven-year-old sister went so far as to say: 'If it were not for the women in the Catholic Church, I might leave it tomorrow.' Sisters are questioning their hitherto firmly held beliefs. In the words of one thirty-eight-year-old sister:

I am beginning to wonder if the Catholic Church has the fullness of truth. I now see a difference between the church and the kingdom, where before I equated the two. The kingdom is much broader than the church, which at this time is latching onto trivia, for example, whether the entrance hymn at Mass should be finished before the priest reaches the altar.

Several sisters are aware of and troubled by two definite groups within the Catholic Church. A forty-eight-year-old sister elaborated on her thoughts:

There seems only one of two things to do. Either I move out of the church and create my own thing or I stay and try to be my own person within, but not fully accepting the structures. I go to the Eucharist, usually once a week, and when I do go to an institutional church celebration, I feel a battered woman when I come out, because, as a woman and a lay person, I'm psychologically denied all the way down the line. For example, every other institution is working to eliminate non-sexist language, whereas ours, supposedly built on justice and love, is not even conscious it is using sexist language. I'm very reluctant to talk about a divided church or two churches, but there is the institutional church in which the official power of the sacraments resides, and the place where people are really being nourished. In the former I can feel my energy being absolutely drained. Something keeps me going to it, but I am no longer constrained or regulated by what is said and done. I believe the Christian heritage is within the Catholic Church, and I will not be robbed by my heritage so I won't walk out of it.

A forty-seven-year-old sister was more hopeful about the Australian Catholic Church of the future. She said:

Regardless of whatever constraints the bureaucracy may establish to maintain a stable, middle class religious identity, the people in the grassroots thrust have a vision and know what they're on about. They have their own energy and will take over. People are going to take life—not law—into their own hands. If the Catholic Church's institutionalism wants to buy into it, it may be lucky enough to be accepted, otherwise it will become an anachronism. By that I mean the system which ploughs under so many bishops. It's the efforts of the papal curia to control the diplomats in various areas, to appoint conservative bishops, to send out negative messages to bishops who are less traditional. The traditional form of power is with the conservatives in the system, but a new energising power in life is taking shape among the people.

Brothers

Of the brothers interviewed, 32 per cent were satisfied with the effectiveness of the Australian Catholic Church. According to this group, the hierarchy, not so caught up in authoritatively teaching dogma, is friendly and appreciative of the contribution and talents of the laity, while, so said a brother in his thirties, most secular clergy are 'extraordinarily effective and giving incalculable service'. These brothers see the church as especially effective in the education and hospital areas. They particularly noted the effectiveness of the St Vincent de Paul Society. Possibly with tongue in cheek, a brother in his late thirties remarked: 'They reckon the motor car is 5 per cent efficient and that does a bloody good job. The Catholic Church is something like that.'

The remaining brothers were more critical. These regarded the hierarchy's reluctance to delegate as one of the main obstacles preventing the effectiveness of the church: a brother in his late forties hoped that bishops would soon rely on the expertise of others in areas such as his own, that of social work. Church leaders, according to several brothers, take too low a profile. They should be quick to speak where necessary against government actions, and not to continue to skirt around the problem of justice. One brother suggested that church statements should be given on television and radio as well as in papers; also, he would like church leaders to be on talk-back shows. He continued: 'I feel clergy are frightened to act and run the risk of mistakes, because they don't want to tarnish the Catholic Church as a sacred institution. Justice is being overlooked for the sake of the dignity of the church.' Another brother commented: 'In some areas the church seems unable to give positive assistance to people. There seem no answers for those victims of broken marriages who cannot openly practise their faith. They are outcasts.'

> Too often [said a thirty-year-old brother] the church moves too slowly against negative influences. Often it sees a problem and has to go through a committee system to devise a philosophy before an approach can begin. People in need are left on their own too long, and the problem becomes almost too large to handle before the church becomes aware of it. That's happened in the case of the unemployed and of the youth.

One brother in his seventies made a comparison:

> The Lutherans, the Uniting Church and the Church of England are following the teachings of Vatican Council more closely than the Catholic Church. The Australian Catholic Church hasn't yet got around to making an authentic response to the good news in its own environment and in its own cultural patterns.

The brothers were particularly vocal at what they call the plight of young people once they leave school. One in his forties commented: 'We've got some good things going at school, religion wise, but the kid goes from that atmosphere to a parish church that hasn't a community spirit. At parish

level we lose touch with them.'
A thirty-year-old brother explained:

> Liturgical reform is very slow. An imbalance is presented to the
> kids. We ask them to go to a celebration of a mystery which is
> central to a believing community and they get thirty minutes
> sermon, fifteen minutes of eucharistic prayer. The ceremony at
> Mass is not highlighting the centrality of the mystery.

A thirty-six-year-old brother knows young people struggling
to identify with the Catholic Church: 'They go from church to
church trying to find meaningful liturgy.' He mentioned one
church where the youth are encouraged to be involved and
create their own liturgy on a Sunday with the result that a lot
are attracted. A brother in his late fifties said: 'I don't blame
them opting out of church where the liturgy is dead. At one I
attended, prayers after holy communion that were said fifty
years ago were read out.'

The youth, according to several brothers, ignore the Catholic
Church's teachings on sexual morality as largely irrelevant,
and the church has not come to grips with this situation. A
brother in his thirties does not believe young people have lost
their faith, they are simply no longer expressing it in the way
previously expected of them: 'They have accepted a Christian
way of living, and they are obviously questioning and thinking
about God and their relationship with him.' Three other
brothers support this view that we can no longer equate a
good Catholic with Sunday Mass attendance. 'If you use a
yardstick such as Mass attendance,' remarked one in his
forties, 'the Catholic Church has been a dismal failure in
recent years. But that's according to the old definition of a
Catholic, which was the definition of a Catholic Irishman.'
Australians, he believes, have been too closely tethered to the
Irish Catholic Church and its expectations.

Priests

Just under half the religious priests accepted the Catholic
Church as they see it operating in Australia. Their reasons,
such as that given by a priest in his twenties, were based on
faith: 'If we believe that it is founded by Christ, then we must

say it is a force for good in society. Once policies have been made and directives given we have to go along with them despite our personal opinions.' A priest in his late forties realistically commented: 'Christ limited what he could have done by inserting himself into a specific historical and geographical context and he still works through the limitations of a human church.' A priest in his early fifties said: 'I don't see anything else able to take the place of the institutional Church.' A priest in his late sixties talked about bureaucracy, a result of institutionalism:

> Bureaucracy in itself is not a bad thing and new bureaucracies, for example social welfare, are developing within the church. One of our challenges is how to evangelise bureaucracy, to make Gospel values impregnate the structures. It simply has to be done.

In defence of the institutional church, two priests pointed to Catholic schools as the major achievement in Australia. One saw the means as important as the objective:

> As an institution, the Australian Catholic Church provided the Catholic school system. It gave the church a definite objective. It demanded and got heroism from religious teachers and from the laity who supplied the finance, and it socially uplifted a group that was on the bottom of the social scale.

Some priests within this first group briefly offered con-structive criticism of the existing institution, the most common being that the clergy must encourage the laity to participate more in church activities. One wanted more power given to episcopal conferences, because those living in a specific area are more knowledgeable about any one of its issues. A priest in his mid-thirties was alone in his wholehearted approval of the institutional Catholic Church:

> Fifty years ago we were the radicals and a threat to the stability of Australia. Today we belong to the Anglican–Uniting Church group. The Catholic Church is very much part of Australian society and has access to influence and power in the country . . . Catholicism has been made accessible to lay people, and there

are lay people able to make a real contribution. We have broken out of the clerical cocoon we had been in for one hundred years.

In direct contrast with this first group, a slight majority of priests were specifically and often insistently critical of the institutional Catholic Church in Australia. A forty-nine-year-old commented on priests in general:

> The lives of a lot of religious and diocesan priests don't speak to people. The priests are in the pulpit, beefing out at people telling them what to do, pre-occupying them with money, structures and building churches. It's not an image people are interested in. Religious priests are still breaking out of structures and an education no longer appropriate for today . . . we're out of touch.

This out-of-touch theme dominates the replies of this second group of priests. They shared the frustration of a priest in his mid-thirties:

> We need to admit the way things are in the world around us and in our parishes and to start searching for authentic answers to the questions that arise. Perhaps the questions are too big for our leaders who still worry about what days should be holy days of obligation.

A fifty-year-old expressed his opinion:

> I am wondering is the Catholic Church of today really a vehicle of evangelising the masses who are not churchgoers. If there is a major event — for example, the Pope visiting Australia — people will be talking about it. That is a negative thing. It is not the church going out there, and I don't know how the church can get into the market square, right there where people are working and enjoying themselves.

He mentioned what others also recognised as a major weakness.

> This is because we don't really recognise the people as the Catholic Church. The clergy are not telling the people they are the church and apostles. There are some lay people who are well informed through their own study, but they are in the minority.

A thirty-six-year-old priest underlined a source of the weakness:

The church is struggling to invite active participation from the laity, but can't succeed, as the existing structures won't permit it. Many parish priests, because of who they are, won't allow full participation from the laity, even though they set up parish councils and committees. Unless the laity actually experience decision-making and then carry those decisions through, the church will continue to decline.

Hence, as another priest said: 'The Australian Catholic Church has a lot of dying to do before new life comes to the surface.'

Several priests recognise signs of new life emerging, not from the institutional church, but, as a thirty-six-year-old priest remarked, from small groups of enthusiastic people who are wanting a deeper commitment to God, a good environment for their children and close community ties. A priest in his late forties said:

Jesus' notion of church was probably those who loved God and their neighbour, so the young people who don't go to church yet are caring do belong to the Catholic Church. If Jesus came back today, I think a lot of people who go to church wouldn't be able to identify with him. In twenty years it will be the young generation who will be leading Catholics and they might develop a new thing.

A priest in his mid-fifties would like a bishop to be a pastor, not an administrator, whose priority would be to know the priests in his diocese. He hopes that, as a result, priests would then be more pastoral and at the service of the people. He, too, deplored the huge resource of educated laity left doing little within the Catholic Church. A number of priests believed that the structural framework of the church was the main obstacle preventing its effectiveness. A priest in his early sixties had widesweeping reforms in mind:

The whole organisation of the church will have to go. A certain metropolitan bishop is the head of his community, yet priests have told me they don't know him. There should be more bishops and a priest for about fifty people. This would mean ordaining men and women, married and single. And they'd have to have a different outlook from today's priests, who don't want to give any power to anyone, especially women.

A priest in his late sixties offered principles for a new concept of church:

> The parish is non-functional at the present time and is breaking down as the number of clergy decreases. We have to move against the present thinking that the minimum requirement for a group of Catholics is one priest and one church. That's capital-intensive ministry and the poor are therefore disadvantaged. We should no longer expect the priest to be the expert in every area. That's dysfunctional today. I agree with the Asian bishops that the essence of priestly ministry is the maintenance and co-ordination of charisms before any sacramental activity. The first obligation of anyone in authority in the church is to identify those who have the various charisms or gifts of ministry. It's ridiculous to expect every man who is ordained to have leadership qualities. We should be using lay people who have already demonstrated leadership in the community and give them some ongoing formation so that they can take leading roles within a parish.

Conclusion

Where religious men were more worried about the church's organisational structure and lack of adaptation to changing society, religious women were more concerned about the effects of the institutional church on individual people, mainly women, in difficult situations. The institutional church, according to some sisters, is failing to show them practical compassion and understanding. The principle enunciated by a thirty-six-year-old sister is that of many others:

> I have to be careful to listen, not to judge. For example, it would be wrong for me with my beliefs to have an abortion, but I don't know whether it would be wrong for someone else. I wouldn't know what a particular woman has gone through. Certainly, the church must offer the ideal, but it should remember that Christ never judged, so what right has it to do so?

174

What emerged from this study was the realisation that at least a very significant number of Catholic laity are no longer content to accept without question the dictates and opinions of those in the institutional church. Some sisters refer to a widening division between two groups within the church. As a fifty-seven-year-old sister said:

> The church has already changed. No matter what the boys at the top say, change is happening, and it has happened among people full of the spirit of God. The teaching church has to listen to the voice of the living church and listen to it as God speaking.

Better educated than their parents, many laity are in the process of reshaping the old definition of Australian Catholics who went to Sunday Mass and obeyed what was given to them as the laws of the church. A thirty-nine-year-old sister gave her definition of the new Catholic outside the terms of an institutional church: 'A Catholic is someone who sees the signs of the Lord in human life.' The laity are realising the ideal is not always humanly possible, and when people have to choose the lesser of two evils in a particular situation, they should receive understanding and acceptance, not rejection. As a forty-seven-year-old sister commented: 'At the moment, the emphasis is more on the system than on the people who should be served by the system.' Although religious men and women are aware of the growing confidence and sense of responsibility among sections of the laity, they do not at present envisage themselves spearheading a lay movement that may radically change the present Australian Catholic Church.

The future of religious life

*O*ne undeniable fact — young men and women are not entering religious congregations — appears to prove that the religious life of today, recognisable still as that of thirty years ago, is gradually dying. Young people evidently do not see it as relevant. Whether the existing religious life has within it seeds of new growth is debatable. If it has, then we must look for changes within religious men and women themselves, because change in personal values and attitudes will eventually determine change in ministry and in lifestyle and, finally, produce a completely new form of religious life.

Change, valid and radical, is the only hope for the future of religious life. This chapter, therefore, examines values, beliefs and attitudes of religious men and women, some of whom are no longer holding to those of thirty years ago. Those with changing views are finding difficulty in coping with lingering remnants of the religious life they once accepted. If there is a future for religious life, we must listen to this minority. And, at this stage, a pertinent question can be asked: why do men and women remain in a religious life that, for the majority, is vastly different from the one they chose at time of entering? More importantly, are there men and women presently wondering if they will leave religious life and, if so, what reasons lie behind their pondering?

Decisions to stay

Sisters

The simple answer to the first question is that the great majority of religious are happy to remain in the religious life they are now leading. This in itself indicates that at least a considerable number of religious do not want or expect future change. Of the sisters interviewed, 72 per cent are fully committed to their vocation and cannot foresee they will ever leave. The greater number of sisters echo the statement of a fifty-six-year-old sister: 'I believe this is where I am meant to be, and it is my way to God.' The emphasis was on the right-ness for the individual. A few often wished they did not have a religious vocation, usually because the attraction to marriage was strong, but they had no doubts that they were in the right place. As a sixty-five-year-old sister said: 'It would not have been my choice but I know it is God's will for me. I am at home with myself. Any life that gives you that conviction is right for you.' Another sister, aged twenty-nine, said: 'This is where I belong. I can't explain it any other way. I can look at a hundred things and say I should leave because of them, but it wouldn't be right for me.'

Others, like a fifty-eight-year-old sister, stress their appreciation of benefits within religious life: 'Nowhere else would one find the same opportunities for growth in faith, hope and love as one does in religious life. The individual has only to take advantage of them.'

A forty-six-year-old sister values her original commitment:

> Commitment is important to me. At one stage I thought, 'If only the puddings are going to stay, how can I survive here?' Which isn't too nice a way of putting it. Regardless of who stays or who doesn't, there is such a breadth of vision and of service in religious life it is worth handing on the spirit. One reason I stay is to hand on this baton, if for nothing else.

Sisters in this group feel they could not be happy other than in religious life.

A smaller proportion of sisters explicitly stated they were in religious life because they sought a relationship with God that they as individuals could find only within it. A forty-four-year-old sister claimed: 'The worst thing that could happen to me would be separation from God. For me, religious life is the only way to have my relationship with God. It is where I am most fully who I am supposed to be.' Or, as a forty-eight-year-old sister said: 'I want to give myself as fully as possible to God and this is the only way I can do it.' A few sisters link their relationship with God to relationship with people. 'I want to be a loving person for others,' a thirty-seven-year-old sister stated. 'My relationship with God grows out of that relationship with others.' Most sisters emphasising relationship with God as a prime motive for remaining in religious life also emphasised the importance of the support a community gives to them: they can see themselves operating only within a group. A twenty-five-year-old sister with temporary vows tried to explain why she remains in religious life:

I find it very difficult to home in on why I entered and why I remain. I don't like the explanation that religious life frees you to be of service to people—it's a consequence, but not a reason for me. My reason is caught up with faith, with relationship with God—a gut feeling that tells me I belong here even though, intellectually, it doesn't make sense.

Although presently content with their vocation, 12 per cent of sisters frankly acknowledged that they might in the future decide to leave religious life. As a forty-eight-year-old sister said: 'I'm not closing off my option to leave.' A further 16 per cent of the sisters interviewed, all under fifty years of age, are presently questioning from a variety of reasons whether they will remain in religious life. A forty-two-year-old sister is convinced she has a religious vocation, but, as a member of an aged congregation, she finds great difficulties in community life.

I want to stay because it is tied up with my desire to give myself completely to God; I feel called to that. Yet I am wondering how I can continue to fit in with the congregation as it is today. The communities I have lived in have had a majority of older sisters and they see me as someone with different ideas and values. I often feel guilty. I want to be a religious, and today that means living in community as it is now. I am hoping that the concept of community will change so that I can live alone with regular contact with a community. Otherwise, I may have to leave.

A forty-three-year-old sister is wondering why she remains in religious life, especially as she has seen many women more gifted and more prayerful than herself leave: there is a distinct possibility she will leave religious life soon. A fifty-year-old sister has no doubts about her own call, but does not know whether she will continue to commit herself to a congregation in which she does not see the majority of sisters striving for ideals.

A thirty-six-year-old sister also questioned religious life as she knows it in her own congregation, not her own call to give her life to God.

> The commitment I made originally was true. I believe in commitments and I am not willing to give up lightly the investment of all my years in religious life. They count for something. And, at the moment, I can't see any alternative that's better than the mess I'm in. I do not see anyone outside religious life who has it all sewn up any better. At least we are striving to share a common ideal. For me, meaning is very important in life and I haven't found any other way of achieving that meaning in my life that is better than what I have at the moment. But then I am living in a small community and we are living a lifestyle different from the traditional. I could not return to traditional lifestyle.

A sister in her early thirties is trying to keep her vocation.

> I stay because I am not sure if it would be the right thing for me to go. I'm still searching. I feel a bit schizophrenic about talking about why I might leave, because I make plans around my staying. It is in moments of solitude, when my own doubts about my reasons for entering and remaining surface that I feel phoney. I have my doubts about my honesty in staying.

Another sister who is in her early forties is struggling with a decision.

> I am always hoping the next year will be better. I could survive as long as I have the freedom to do my own thing and as long as I don't get too much into the centre of the congregation: I don't want to be in any role where I have to toe the party line. I am at home and can relax with the sisters, but I don't want any part of the official government in religious life.

For over two years a forty-year-old sister has been rethinking her vocation:

> I'm trying to be realistic. At my age it is a bit late to begin another life, to begin a family life. But I don't feel there is a niche for me in my congregation. I don't like teaching, which is our main ministry, and I'm uncertain as to what work I can do. I've also unfortunately

been in a community that was split in two over the style of religious life. I'm in the process of becoming more my own person and that is tied up with finding out where I can be.

Brothers

Not one brother interviewed indicated that he was re-examining his vocation. The majority exuded a genuine enjoyment of religious life, and many actually admitted that they did enjoy it. At one or other period of their lives 52 per cent of brothers had looked seriously at the possibility of leaving their congregations. They attributed their doubts to a crisis point: pressure of work, problems with community, family illness or death. A few brothers had daydreamed of advantages they would enjoy as laymen, but, as one wryly put it, no more seriously than the happily married man daydreams about his secretary. Most stay in religious life because, in the words of a brother in his early forties, 'I want to be here; I believe this is where I am meant to be.' 'The positives', commented another, 'outweigh the negatives.'

Besides feeling they were in the right niche, other brothers added that they were convinced their work or ministry was very worthwhile. A forty-three-year-old brother sees his commitment to his congregation as 'a contract with God for better or for worse. I promised for ever.' As a thirty-seven-year-old brother said: 'If I walked out today, I would be walking out on something.' Only a fifty-six-year-old brother spoke in such terms as: 'The feeling that the Lord has drawn me into religious life has never left me.'

Priests

Among the priests 44 per cent have never doubted their vocation, 40 per cent have doubted only at times of crisis. So 84 per cent of priests are happy in their vocation, and their reasons are summed up in two comments. A fifty-nine-year-old priest said: 'I really love my life. I like my prayers and I enjoy helping people. There's no other option for me.' The other comment was given by a forty-six-year-old:

I really believe God has called me to my particular congregation,

182

and I am happily responding to that call. It sounds pretty trite, but that's what I believe. It's never crossed my mind to leave.

The remaining 16 per cent are presently grappling with the question of their vocation. One in his late twenties explained his difficulties:

I'm very much aware of the great good people are doing in the world, and I'm aware we religious are not living as radically as we could be. There seems to be as many reasons for going as for staying. I think it's very easy as a religious not to develop or to have as meaningful a life as a lay person. All the signs are that I am suited to this life, and I could be comfortable with that, but challenges come from outside religious life and it's then I have serious doubts as to its relevance.

Another priest in his early thirties is more emotionally involved in his problem:

I've actually quite violently cursed God for a lonely life in religion. Yet I know I can decide to leave. Sometimes I think I'd like to wander for a couple of years just to see what happens. I'm waiting for something to let me know what I'll do.

The crisis in his religious vocation involves a wider issue for a priest in his mid-thirties.

A major question for me is about the nature of the church. I think the structures of the church have made it difficult for its members to be free. The church represses so much of what makes us human individuals and encourages a passivity in us. So I'm questioning what the church is doing to me. On the other hand, I feel that if I left the priesthood I would inflict hurt on my parents, friends and the religious I've lived with, and I have great difficulty in coping with that, even though it's a very poor motivation for staying. I realise I am developing as a person in my congregation, but, as I do, I become more aware of the restrictions, the shackles, so I guess the question is whether my continual growth is possible where I am. I'm not up to a decision point yet.

All religious

From information supplied in interviews it is only possible to make a general observation that men and women intending to remain in their religious congregations are doing so because they feel comfortable within them, comfortable in the sense that they know it is the place for them, their niche or home. Similarly, one can only generalise that those men and women wondering if they will remain in religious life feel alien or unable to develop their human potential within their congregations.

Without further research it is impossible to determine to what extent the brothers' greater concentration on and involvement with the one ministry of schools is responsible for their greater satisfaction with religious life, but this is certainly a factor unique to the brothers. Religious priests have a variety of reasons for questioning their vocation, but there is a strong impression that their community life is not as supportive as those of other religious. Judging from the results of this study, religious women are the yeast in the ferment of change in religious life. In particular, one notes those sisters wondering not whether they will, but whether they can, remain in religious life and, more importantly, those sisters who are actually working directly or indirectly for radical changes. The latter seem mainly the sisters who live in small communities in which their ministry determines their lifestyle, the sisters who wish to be, and are, identified with lay people beside whom they work, the sisters who have become involved in what might be termed non-religious areas, for example, petitioning town councils to redress injustices of the minority within their locality.

Values, attitudes and beliefs

Sisters

Values, attitudes and beliefs are important in determining the direction of any group of people; especially is this true for religious congregations. To tap into some of these, I asked those I interviewed about their image of God, ideals of a religious and the qualities in religious people they knew and admired.

The original image of God for 38 per cent of sisters was that of a benevolent, caring God. A forty-seven-year-old sister in this group had what she smilingly termed a romantic image of God, 'the equivalent of a virile Robert Redford'. The remaining 62 per cent had first seen God as authoritarian, a judge in the sky, someone, as a thirty-seven-year-old sister explained, 'who cracked the whip if I stepped out of line'. For many, religious life strengthened this image: 'In the novitiate he also became a clock God,' said a fifty-six-year-old sister, 'one who expected me to be 110 per cent perfect all the time.' For all sisters, God has become closer and more real; 'a loving father' was the most commonly used description. The image of God as a potter was often implicitly present. A twenty-nine-year-old sister spoke about 'a gentle, joyful, relaxed God, someone who is compassionate and can also laugh with you'. The majority of sisters felt an evident relief that their God no longer expected perfection from them: 'I did not believe he would ever forgive me some of my mistakes,' confessed a sister in her late thirties. As a forty-eight-year-old sister explained: 'Doing the right thing is no longer the criterion of his approval of me.' Some, like a seventy-two-year-old sister, are comfortably familiar with God: 'Even when I am playing cards,' she said, 'I will say, "Come on, Lord, I want a good hand this time."'

Practising yoga has helped a seventy-eight-year-old sister to arrive at a quiet and more continual presence of God. 'There was a time', she said, 'when I was searching for God. Now he is continually with me.' Because they have become more aware of the transcendental God, sixteen sisters discussed the futility of trying to contain him within specific characteristics. A sister aged forty tried to explain:

> I am not sure how I see God now. All I know is that I can no longer put him into a box and label him. I am coming to a different understanding of God, moving from seeing him as a person to feeling him as a presence. When I was formerly aware of his presence it was a presence imposed from outside. Whereas now I understand him coming from within life. I don't know if that makes sense — I'm really grappling with it myself.

Ten sisters agreed with a thirty-eight-year-old sister when she said: 'Whenever God comes to mind I think of Jesus in terms of his humanity. He has always been central for me, a personal friend.' A fifty-year-old sister has come to realise that Christ was very radical in his lifetime: 'I have to stop and wonder if I have made him into a God that suits my particular way of looking at things. I'm finding this disturbing, as it will demand rather drastic changes in me.'

Other sisters have linked their concept of God specifically with people. A fifty-eight-year-old sister is typical of and speaks for this group. The people among whom she lives and works, financially deprived in a struggling suburb, largely ignorant of basic living and communication skills, have given her another facet to a loving God:

God is a tough personality who expects his people to fight for change. He wants us real in our situation whatever that is. When I eventually meet him, he will say to me, 'There was an awful lot of bull-shit in what you did.'

She is the sister who also said: 'It is as important to be a good citizen as to be a good Christian. And that means standing beside people and fighting for their rights.'

Of the sisters, 38 per cent find their main support in God and prayer. Although many expressed a deep appreciation for the prayers of the church, formalised prayers are not popular with the sisters. A sixty-year-old sister admitted that she can no longer pray from the Gospels as the reading distracts her from a deeper prayer level. A number of sisters speak to God in their hearts, while others, as a fifty-three-year-old said, 'Just sit with him.' And 40 per cent of sisters rely on both prayer and people — friends, family and sisters in community. The remaining 22 per cent rely on people for support, especially on those who share their own vision: 'I am appreciating more and more', remarked a forty-four-year-old sister, 'the support people can offer me. I am touched by their courage, strength and desire to do good.' A fifty-two-year-old sister shares what she thinks and does with her family: 'I am the youngest of eight children, and they're still protective of me as the baby of the family.' Another sister finds more support from an elderly sister within her congregation: 'After I speak to her I come away feeling three inches taller. She is so happy in herself and she always affirms me. It acts as refuelling for me.'

When asked what for them were the ideals of a religious, 77 per cent of sisters answered in language associated only with the church ard religious life. Complete perfection in the terms of traditional Christian writers appeared to be the ideal. A seventy-three-year-old sister said: 'A religious should do the best she can in her work, offering it to Jesus for her own sanctification, for the salvation of souls in Purgatory and for a world that has forgotten to pray.'

A fifty-seven-year-old sister gave her ideal: 'A religious should be a true spouse of Christ, his beloved, and should bring forth souls for the kingdom.' A younger sister, aged forty-four years, gave much the same definition: 'A religious should have a relationship with God, a sense of what community life means and should be involved in apostolic work within the church.'

Their replies are typical of the others in this group. Of the sisters, 5 per cent combined generalised Christian terminology with specific human qualities. An example is the definition given by a forty-seven-year-old sister: 'A religious should have a close relationship with God and be prayerful. She must be authentic; that is, to be what she seems. She should also be tolerant, accepting people as they are.' The remaining 18 per cent used attributes to describe the ideal that is appropriate for any human being, Christian or atheist. A sister in her seventies spoke of a loving, patient and accepting person who lived these qualities in a low-key style. A forty-six-year-old sister said:

> The ideal religious relates to people as the woman she is, not out of a role. She's in touch with her own humanity and weakness so she can understand weakness in others and allows them to see hers. She is happy for the people for whom she works to minister to her as much as she ministers to them. She accepts people as they are without trying to change them with her particular ideas of improvement.

When a fifty-year-old sister commented that the ideals of any good human being are basically those of a religious, she spoke for many other sisters.

When sisters were asked what were the qualities of the religious people whom they admired, not one completely restricted herself to the terminology associated with the church and religious life. Each chose a religious because of what that particular person had meant and had done for her or for others she knew. Of the sisters interviewed, 63 per cent described very lovable human qualities, among which joy in life and generosity were prominent. A forty-six-year-old sister spoke about the qualities of steadfastness, courage, humour and the capacity to continue as a loving person in a loveless environment. A fifty-five-year-old sister recalled her days as a novice when she met a sister she came to love and admire, and who in her late eighties was confined to a wheelchair.

> She had great compassion and generosity of spirit with a beautiful sense of humour. Her joy in the small things of life attracted me. I had the privilege of wheeling her to Mass every day and she would urge me, 'Faster, sister, faster!' so that I would race her along the verandas to give her a thrill, much to the horror of other senior sisters.

Selflessness, active interest in and loving concern for others were common qualities mentioned. A forty-five-year-old sister was influenced as a boarder by one particular sister.

> She worked in our boarding school, and I noticed that, at night, in her spare time, she would assist youngsters who were finding school work difficult. She took a special interest in country children who came to board. She seemed to have some idea of what it cost those youngsters to be away from home.

Other most frequently mentioned qualities were: integrity, gentleness, honesty, warmth, approachability, openness, courage, and the ability to forgive and encourage. A thirty-seven-year-old sister admired religious 'who had vision and weren't afraid to change, women who had the courage to take risks.' The remaining 37 per cent emphasised the above qualities, but also included qualities normally linked with religious life. With rare exceptions, these were: trust in God, love of God, great faith and enthusiasm for Gospel values.

There is an anomaly here. Intellectually, the majority of sisters ascribe to the traditional ideals of a religious, ideals placed before them when they entered religious life. They emphasise what are sometimes called spiritual values: love of God, obedience to the religious rule, prayerfulness. However, when asked what had attracted them to specific religious, 63 per cent had looked only at other qualities, very human, appealing qualities and even the 37 per cent who had included religious values were more interested in basic human values. This, of course, proves that, within tightly structured and restricted religious lifestyle, some individuals were able to develop as lovable, admirable human beings. For most sisters, however, there still appears a dichotomy between the head and the heart that may be connected to the theology of past years in which the soul and body, the spiritual and material, were distinctly separated. Such a dichotomy may be related to the lack of vocations today and to younger sisters questioning whether they can remain in religious life. The crux may be whether the desire of many sisters to be seen as lay women with ordinary human qualities can be accomplished within the existing religious framework. Speaking for these sisters, a thirty-six-year-old spelt out her attitude:

I admire most what I call 'humanness'; none of this out-of-the-world pious veneer that I have met in some religious people which I find sickly sweet and which has nothing to do with every day life. Humanness for me means trying to get in touch with the human person of Jesus. The greatest thing anyone can do is to live life as humanly as he did. I want to be open to whatever life brings me. I experience limitations as a human being, and I really want to be able to accept them and live with them. I don't want to live in some sort of unreal way that tries to blot out hurt or tragedy or joy. I want to be real enough to own who I am and what that means. I am very limited with a lot of faults, but I want to live within that, to live without a mask, to take myself seriously, but not too seriously.

Brothers

From their original image of God as an all-seeing judge, a tyrant who punished, or as some vague, elderly gentleman who was almost a magician, the majority of brothers now envisage a loving, compassionate father and friend, on whom they trustingly depend. A minority claimed that there has been little basic change in their first image of God as father. The fatherhood concept of God is common to brothers, and they no longer feel they must earn his affection — it is recognised as a gift. A brother in his early seventies finds that, as he grows older, the more indefinable God becomes for him:

> I now see the old absolute statements about God in the catechism as feeble attempts by men to contain God in a certain philosophy. I keep forming new models, then realising I am restricting him. God is escaping from all the models I make for him.

This brother is now aware that Christianity has not a monopoly on God, and he admires the Aborigines, wholistic in their thinking, who experience God in the world in which they live. Other brothers have also lost a definite image of God. A brother in his mid-thirties acknowledges God as presence with power, one who loves people into existence: another in his fifties recognises him in people, especially within a loving family group. A brother in his forties said that Jesus was for him the personification of the mystery of God. He was one in the 40 per cent of brothers who have a closer relationship with Jesus than with the God of the Trinity. All brothers accepted Jesus as friend and guide because, as a brother in his sixties said: 'He is a man and he suffered just as I do.' A brother in his fifties admitted:

> Sometimes I won't let him come close to me. I'm not always prepared to see him in people. Some old bloke comes around for a feed and I think, 'Ah, crikey, not again.' If I were fair dinkum, I would see God there in that man. I'm not too good yet at that kind of thing.

Prayer, especially that based on the Gospels, is important for all brothers. At times of personal prayer, most have moved from saying formalised prayers to being silent in the presence of God. As a brother in his late thirties remarked, 'For me, God is an experience.' Although recognising the support of people, 72 per cent of brothers find their main support in prayer. A brother in his twenties said that his quietly growing prayer life 'gives a centre to things' and one in his forties remarked: 'I am convinced that, despite the evidence that everything is going wrong, time will show it isn't. In prayer I find that conviction and a peace which keeps me going.' Without specifically mentioning prayer, the remaining brothers emphasised their appreciation for and dependence on the support of their brothers in community, friends and family.

Of the brothers, 32 per cent couched their ideals of a religious in wholly spiritual terms. Where one spoke only of living out the counsels of Christ and entering more fully into the paschal mystery, the others included a responsibility for people. For example, a forty-year-old brother said: 'A religious must live out the Gospel values so that people can actually see that there is more to life than becoming immersed in material values.' That the brothers' spirituality has a decidedly practical base is further borne out by 56 per cent who combined spiritual with human qualities when they described their ideals of a religious. When a forty-one-year-old brother talked about his ideal, his remarks were typical of this group:

I want to be a person of prayer, to be one who lives in and contributes to community and to be a witness of hope and of a Christian life for people. With all that idealism, a religious has to be sane and able to enjoy life as it is. If you get all those high falutin' spiritual ideas and float off into the clouds, you should give religious life away. You must be very much down to earth.

And as a fifty-nine-year-old brother said:

A religious should see the Lord as priority No. 1 and be committed to his prayer life. He should relate well with and support people. He should live up to the expectations of his congregation and of God, yet he should not be starry-eyed; there will be many difficulties in coping with religious life.

The remaining brothers, 12 per cent, concentrated on very human qualities. Selflessness was the common ideal, yet

191

practical common sense again was to the fore: a thirty-six-year-old brother commented that selflessness did not mean he was to have no time for himself and his own development. Other qualities mentioned were humility, compassion, approachability and tolerance. Brothers are more at home with their ideals than are other religious. Expecting fallibility and so having no undue worries about mistakes along the way, they emphasise the humour and joy in life. As a forty-three-year-old brother said: 'A religious should be happy and fulfilled, yet if he works for that, he'll miss the boat.'

The qualities brothers admired in specific religious were very similar in spirit to their concept of ideals. So 60 per cent linked spiritual and human qualities. A thirty-five-year-old brother spoke of his admiration for a brother nearing seventy:

> He is still enthusiastic and interested in the kids, shares jokes with them. He's friendly and just nice. A great contributor to community life and a great man to have around—a giving man. He's also genuinely faithful to religious life in a manly way.

A thirty-nine-year-old brother referred to another older man:

> He has this passion for teaching religious education; he's interested, not in laws, but in helping people develop themselves fully. While being realistic, he affirms and encourages people. He has this deep understanding of what it is to be human yet he demands the best from people.

Of the brothers, 40 per cent referred to human qualities in the religious they admire. Again there is an emphasis on joy in life, living life to the full, a magnanimity of spirit. A sixty-four-year-old brother marvelled at changes he has seen in brothers: 'We had been taught to be very reserved, very aloof, especially with women. Now that has changed. Gentleness, tenderness and concern for others are visible qualities in many of us.' One brother in his forties summed up what the great majority implied in their description of those they admire: 'They are real people—genuine—with no pretence. They stand by what they believe in.'

Priests

A seventy-year-old priest remembers his early image of God as 'a huge painted eye that saw everything'. A forty-nine-year-old recalls him as 'a big ogre, a punishing corrector'. Most had less dramatic images: their early God was a just judge to whom they were accountable, or an impersonal father-figure who left it to his followers to make whatever contact they could with him. Three had seen him as leader and guide. For a thirty-six-year-old priest it has been 'a shattering of many God images along the way'. Formerly he had seen him as a distant God.

> Gradually I came to understand that he was distant to allow me responsibility to grow without his dominating me by law or by blinding me with his light. I understand now the powerlessness of Jesus. I don't want a God who directs my life; I want him close to me. My meditation is related to a sense of intimacy with God. It's like emptying everything out and just being present to him and him being present to me.

A fifty-nine-year-old priest said: 'When I was young, I always saw myself doing things for God. Now I feel God is doing things in me. He is no longer outside myself but deep inside me.'

Several priests have found a caring God through their own weakness and sometimes sinfulness. One in his thirties explained:

> I used to be a perfect religious on my own terms, because I did everything that was expected of me quite happily. I was able to control myself and direct my life. I was a real tough nut until I found I could not control my desires. There was the whole question of masturbation—this was a mortal sin and blotted the copybook. Then I read that part in St Paul where he rejoices in his weakness and I found that very consoling. Now I believe that no matter what I do, he will not desert me. He mightn't agree with what I'm doing, but he won't desert me.

A priest twenty years older had come to the same conclusion: 'I can do anything I like, and God will still love me. Sin hurts me more than it bothers God. I have a growing sense of gratitude towards God as I appreciate more my giftedness.' Most priests feel close to a very loving, personal God. As a sixty-four-year-old priest said: 'He is one who understands me.'

Without ignoring the importance of prayer, 56 per cent of priests rely on people for their main support — family, friends and their community. A fifty-six-year-old priest said:

> Intellectually I guess prayer is my main support, but emotionally I find it in others who love and appreciate me. Spiritual experiences are very supportive, but I tend now to look more carefully at the human experiences because I've neglected them in the past, thinking that I could live happily without them. When I've had a good experience with somebody or somebody has praised me genuinely, that is very supportive.

Others have a variety of support factors in their lives. Two priests in their sixties stated that they do not depend on people. One spoke for the two of them: 'If you understand the dignity and responsibility of the position of the priesthood, then it is easier to live up to it.' Others rely solely on God and prayer. A thirty-five-year-old priest explained his two main supports:

> I have a firm belief and trust in Divine Providence. The other support is myself. I like myself. It is good to be alive. My work helps me to feel worthwhile, but I no longer rely so heavily on the need to be doing something to feel good.

In outlining their ideal of a religious, 32 per cent of priests used language associated with spiritual writers and lecturers of thirty years ago to describe the way in which, in their opinion, religious life should be lived. A typical example is that given by a priest in his early seventies:

> Religious should live their vows in community and according to gospel maxims. They should be outgoing leaders of the faithful and dedicate their time and abilities to the particular work of their community.

A few priests were quick to add that the Catholic Church needed the variety of spirituality that the various congregations offer to their members: 'A religious', said a fifty-nine-year-old, 'puts the Gospel values into practice according to his congregation's rule of life and the charism of his founder.' As a group, priests emphasised the witness and service religious should give to lay people. For example, a thirty-six-year-old priest stated:

A religious should be a sign of hope, a sign of the possibility all can grow as people and a sign of God's presence in the world. Others should be able to recognise by the way he lives that he is there to serve them.

The ideals of the remaining 68 per cent are applicable to all Christians, and admirable human qualities dominate. These priests agreed with one in his forties:

Religious are meant to model a quality of Christian living. A Christian life is Christ-centred and witnesses to Gospel values. Religious should be alive, vibrant, happy people who say something by the way they live rather than by words. Their lives should testify to simplicity and be ones of service to others.

Prayerfulness and commitment to the service of people were high on the list of qualities priests admired in religious they have known. A thirty-six-year-old priest recalled an old man he had known:

I think of a priest I admire who lived in a pre-Vatican II world even two years ago—a world to which I could never relate. He lived a very ascetical, rigid life in some ways. But the thing that stood out in this man's life was his closeness to God.

A thirty-five-year-old greatly admired the brothers in his clerical congregation:

They were hard-working, perhaps a bit rough in appearance, but they had a gentleness and a real empathy for others, especially for anyone in trouble. They gave courageous witness in a very ordinary way. I was privy to some of the suffering they encountered at the hands of others through misunderstanding but they had no bitterness; they had an ability to be joyful even in the face of that. They taught me what forgiveness means.

Besides prayerfulness, gentleness was the most frequently mentioned quality, with compassion, generosity, openness and practicality also popular. Most admitted to admiring religious who were, in the words of one priest, 'genuine human beings'. A priest in his late forties recalled one religious whom he admired:

> He was a charming gentleman, a deeply human person. He had a great taste for red wine. It was symbolic of his life. He used to roll life around his mouth like wine, to chuckle about it, savour it and, occasionally, if he didn't like it, to spit it out.

The future

Brothers

How, then, do these religious men and women see and feel about the future for religious life? Of the brothers, 28 per cent believe that declining numbers will continue until their congregations gradually disappear. 'We have done our work in Catholic education in this country,' said a forty-two-year-old brother. 'It can be continued by lay people.' And a brother in his forties commented: 'After all, two-thirds of all congregations have disappeared since the beginning of religious life.' The majority in this group admit with a thirty-five-year-old brother:

> I don't know how I feel about the future. I don't let myself think about it a great deal. I guess changes are happening now as we gradually move out of schools through lack of personnel. For instance, five brothers left us last year, and we haven't had five new brothers for many years.

While the remaining 72 per cent believe or hope that religious life will continue, all are definite that, for this to happen, changes will have to occur. 'It's absolutely essential', asserted a brother in his fifties, 'that we get back to the cutting edge.'

196

He continued:

You can look back to extraordinary religious people of the eighteenth and nineteenth centuries who saw different emerging needs and just plunged in to meet them without fear or any thought of security. Somehow we've got to get back that spirit, and we're reluctant to do it, because our lifestyle has become very comfortable in Australia and to regain that pioneering spirit is going to be very, very difficult. Basically, we don't want to do it and yet it's going to be absolutely essential if we are going to survive.

A few brothers looked to the past to explain the present, thus indicating trends that, if encouraged, could either eliminate or create the future for religious. One said:

We've always adopted the lifestyle of the people we serve and, up to relatively recent times, there was no problem with that, because the people we served were basically working-class Irish Catholics who lived very poor lifestyles. We were marvellously successful in helping them move into middle class by the 1960s, and we walked with them step by step. So now we find ourselves right in the centre of a middle class and, if we stay there, we're doomed to extinction, because that makes us irrelevant to the people who now really need us.

A thirty-five-year-old brother agreed: 'The future has to be more radical—the real problems are in the deprived areas and we need to go there without the structures of schools.' With an exceptionally deep, personal and wide professional knowledge of religious men and women, a brother in his forties acknowledged the difficulties in the way of this radical change:

A lot of religious are struggling with the enormous changes that have already occurred in recent years. Change has thrown their world upside down and some are not coping with life in general. We're suffering the legacy of a somewhat triumphalist approach to life from the fifties and early sixties. Those who taught in schools that were theirs, or who nursed in their own hospitals, or who were parish priests believing the parish was their domain find it hard to cope today in changed conditions. Then, as well, a

197

lot can't handle the rigorous demands of the modern style of community living and of personal responsibility. They can't handle the loneliness that has always been in religious life but which they can't now avoid due to the way we lead our lives as religious. One of the biggest problems is that people tend to think the end of religious life is inevitable, but a lot can really be done.

He did not, however, offer any practical ways for improving the situation. Most brothers therefore believe that for religious life to survive, its lifestyle will need to change and traditional ministries left to the laity. For brothers, it would appear, ministry determines whether religious life will continue. But one brother made a pertinent comment:

> A lot of congregations tend to run the risk of making the mistake of confusing means and ends. For example, how a congregation diversifies in ministry is of secondary importance as to why it's wanting to do that in the first place. To survive, religious have to be sure of priorities, and there is still some confusion among us concerning priorities.

Priests

On the whole, priests are more pessimistic than brothers about the survival of religious life: 44 per cent cannot envisage its continuance, 36 per cent concede that drastic changes need to occur if religious life is to survive, while only 20 per cent are certain of its survival without qualification of that certainty. The objective viewpoint of a priest born in the Philippines taps into the thinking of some Australian priests:

> In Australia, religion is a private business. I find a lack of celebration and joy in religion as it's practised here. The clergy and religious are not prepared to commit themselves in public on social matters. It is not surprising that religion and those associated with it are seen as irrelevant to society as a whole.

Irrelevance is the underlying theme of most priests except those in the 20 per cent group. As a thirty-six-year-old priest said: 'The charism of some congregations is not speaking to our times.' A thirty-four-year-old priest concurred:

Religious life as it stands now, in the way it is now lived, cannot survive. The world is too used to us, so we're nicely categorised and put into a box and the safe Christian life. Religious should be arriving at a realistic authentic faith that is able to transform a culture instead of it being part of the culture.

Far from seeing religious life transforming a culture, a fifty-nine-year-old priest believes that, on the whole, religious have a closed mentality and will not look beyond their congregations: 'They seem to be putting all their energies into preserving themselves.' In his twenties, a young priest spoke on behalf of his generation: 'Young people desire to give everything, but our congregations are not offering them enough challenges.' 'We live too well and are not sufficiently mission-oriented,' said another young priest, unconvinced that religious life will continue.

A priest in his fifties and another in his forties are concerned at what they see as a growing conservatism among religious. 'We're too frightened to face what we perhaps discern,' said the former. 'We're slipping back into many attitudes of the past. Vatican II gave us an impetus, which is slowing down.' The latter remarked: 'I get worried that church authorities want to gather renewal under one form so they can tidy it all up again and control it.'

Hoping and trusting that religious congregations will continue, some priests offered constructive criticism of existing religious life. A sixty-two-year-old priest contributed his opinion:

As we're living, we're not really getting the Gospel preached to us. The pipeline conveying spirituality to us is far too thin. We're out of reality and starved spiritually. We're living more as descendants of celibates than we are of our own fathers and mothers. We have to become more inserted into the normal world. Christianity and the Gospel are too big for this kind of existence we live. We need to be in community with married people, single people and people of other religions so that we can share the Gospel daily on a live-in basis to get the richness of it.

He sees a 'tremendous future' for religious life coming from lay people longing for closer union with God through prayer, and said, 'We may have to get a new definition for religious life.' A seventy-year-old priest also sees the beginning of a new form of religious life among the laity. He referred to lay women he knows working as full-time parish workers and paid by the parish, but never intending to enter a convent.

> Such women working in parish ministry will need some community support and will group together in small groups. Professionally trained people — nurses, guidance officers, teachers — may make a simple promise to live together because active ministry is impossible without prayer and support.

He believes the new religious life will take place outside the existing congregations because, as he said, 'You can't expect older religious to change.'

Most priests foresee that the present trend will continue: there will be a great reduction in the number of religious; they will move out of institutional works and houses into smaller groups with more emphasis on ministry than on community life so that there will be no one model for religious life. Religious life will possibly include those with permanent vows and those who make themselves available for a certain time. A priest in his forties said: 'There will be fewer religious, but they will model a real quality of living so people will say of them, "They're nice people." Religious life will be lived, not separated from people as it once was, but among them.'

A priest in his forties urged congregations to give young people with new ideas a real chance to try them out:

> Older religious [he noted] are too fearful of making mistakes. . . The big question is whether we are going to continue changing quickly enough to relate to all the people looking for spirituality. If we don't, religious life will fade out.

Most priests underlined the urgency for change. A man in his sixties said:

> Congregations founded in reaction to the Reformation, and that applies to most, have a reactionary type of spirituality, which is no longer needed. A spirituality that has a negative outlook on life can't survive. We now see religion far more as an expression of

life and not just spiritual life. Religious life has to become more open with greater physical freedom for members, which involves greater trust and responsibility. People still have a picture of religious being closed in, away from life, and this is one of the greatest obstacles to those who might otherwise consider religious life. A broader mentality is needed. Justice, for example, must be considered on a world scale. Religious should be in the vanguard of change, not trailing a couple of hundred years behind.

Sisters

Of religious women, 83 per cent believe that religious life will continue, but some assert that it will take a vastly different form from that of today. As a seventy-four-year-old sister said: 'Religious life as we know it will die out—its origin, a defensive measure after the Reformation, has already disappeared.' Sisters gave helpful criticism of the existing situation within religious life, helpful because, if read positively, it offers remedies hopefully ensuring a future for religious life. A fifty-nine-year-old sister, for example, pointed out: 'We have concentrated too long on institutional, child-centred ministry, and we have lived away from the centre of the action. We must now move into more adult-centred ministry.'

Sisters must realistically face a religious heritage from past years, a heritage posing problems peculiarly theirs both in present and for future times. A forty-three-year-old brother objectively indicated the basis for them:

> Allowing that all generalisations have their limitations, it is historically true that in Australia the men have always had a certain amount of freedom that was denied women religious, so that, whilst religious life was obviously different from secular life, the difference for male religious was never as great a contrast as that for women. So, when changes came, it required a greater effort for them to bridge the gap between their religious sub-culture and the Australian culture.

From personal experience with sisters in his work, a sixty-seven-year-old priest had this to say:

> With developments after Vatican II, religious women in particular

had a deep sense of having been exploited in the past, of having been humiliated in their formation system, of being interchangeable with anyone else. Their personal identity was denied them. That brought a reaction which needed healing. Some have coped and come to terms with their history; others have been unable to do so.

A thirty-six-year-old sister commented on another result from changes after Vatican II:

In getting out of habits, with changes in structures, religious women have been brought face to face with the fact they are human and this has led to two responses: some have retreated, clinging to the past, and some have really become part of lay people's lives in a real way. Overall, however, I would say that, since the 1970s, the original impulse for change has slowed down. There's a lack of nerve, an uncertainty about our identity that together generates a sense of hopelessness among us.

With such a history it is remarkable that, living with those who appear paralysed by this uncertainty and feeling of hopelessness, there are vital women optimistically grappling with changes that may bring new life to their congregations. Hence, polarisation often results within such congregations. A number of sisters are concerned about these two distinct groups. A sister in her late forties was hopeful that the more vital group will take action.

I see two clearly differentiated streams of religious within most congregations: there are those who are comfortable with the past ideas of what religious life is about and believe that because they once worked very hard, they deserve to do very little now and to be looked after. I see another stream developing—representative ages in this as in the former—of sisters in individual ministries supporting and supported by those in a few institutional ministries. They will move flexibly from one ministry to another, from one lifestyle to another, living in a variety of community compositions.

Far more critical is the situation, however, when individual, enthusiastic sisters feel torn between a responsibility towards those content with the present situation and a responsibility to the future. One such sister said:

I feel trapped. I don't want to let the team down. I have a commitment to them. Yet some are unwilling to move beyond their present stance. That's very evident at our large meetings and assemblies. What can I do? What should I do?

Where once the congregation would elect a number of delegates to regular meetings or chapters to determine guidelines for the future, now all members of most congregations expect to be present and to have equal voice at them. Theoretically good, this does have disadvantages for the group as a whole. The majority may unthinkingly support the views of the currently popular and vocal religious; small groups or cliques may influence decision-making; forward-looking sisters with creative ideas that involve risks may not be heard; and the needs of the congregation as a group, usually voiced by insecure sisters fearful of an uncertain future, may dominate decision-making so that most of the energy of religious is spent on maintaining the congregational system. Sisters from this group frequently asked me whether the results of this study depressed me or caused me concern about the future of religious life. To me the very asking of the question shows an overconcern with religious life as a good in itself. A more pertinent question might have been to ask into what areas would the energies of the sisters best be channelled.

Noting that religious are no longer the vanguard of the Catholic Church, a sister in her forties suggests why, in her opinion, this is so. She contrasts today's laity with today's religious.

The forward movement of the laity is incredible, and what worries me is that the religious are going to lag far behind. It worries me that, for many people, what they perceive as religious life is something from the past and the laity is surging ahead with a vision, a hope, a life of prayer and a vibrancy that so many of our convents lack. I say 'convents' deliberately because I think it is often the convent environment that helps to set a tone of nostalgia for the pre-Vatican II image. It worries me that I see a lack of energy in the young ones as well as in the old. There's a whole atmosphere of tiredness in our convents. Lay people are running a home, doing a job and going to spiritual courses, and we've become navel-gazers.

When asked to what she attributes this lack of energy, she replied:

I think it comes from a loss of their sense of identity, because so much of it was in external trappings and in terms of work. Saying they are tired justifies their slack existence and their low self-esteem. Another cause is boredom. Many religious didn't have to seek a meaning; it was given to them, and they haven't had to reclaim it in a new setting, so they're bored. They're settled into a kind of balance between two worlds — the old world of religion in which they really still have their identity and the more comfortable things the new world offers them. The great pity is that younger religious are being caught up in this. However, I wouldn't want to over-simplify: there are religious with great creative energy, women who have had their Golden Jubilees who are branching out into two or three new ministries.

Herself within this group of creative women religious, a thirty-one-year-old sister attempted to define the new form of religious life: 'If you see religious life as being caught up in God and wanting God to be the centre of your life, then it will always be with us.' Sisters foresee practical changes. Fewer sisters will possibly result in the amalgamation of congregations as well as in smaller communities within congregations. Sisters envisage some mixed communities of married couples, single people and religious of both sexes, some with permanent, others with temporary commitments. A sister in her early forties commented: 'Mixed communities will act as a very vital, enabling factor for ministry.' A forty-five-year-old sister had lived a few years within a community including lay people and noted the advantages of their inclusion:

They were far more challenging than religious. They called a spade a spade. They certainly let you know if they thought you weren't contributing as you should. Religious, on the other hand, are fearful of confrontations.

Religious may also live alone, meeting regularly with others in an identical situation, thus creating a new form of community life. More mobile and flexible, the lifestyle of new communities will vary according to the neighbourhood and ministry of the religious members. That these communities will form an integral part in parish life was taken for granted. A group of three sisters, one of whom was interviewed, takes for granted that community means being part of their neighbourhood community, in the sense that they become involved with local matters. A sister in her thirties enlarged on her vision:

> The significant change in my thinking is that my community must include living as part of a neighbourhood, not just as part of an isolationist group of happy sisters. The future religious community will have to be an integral part of the wider community. We have to move out of our complexes, out of special privileges and aura of being precious into being just ordinary human beings who have given themselves to God and to serving the church as best they can.

A sixty-three-year-old sister shares her vision:

> I see religious infiltrating society rather than influencing it from large institutions. Religious will be far more active on an individual level in the vanguard action within the church and even in society for that's where religious should be.

There was no consensus as to the place of community within future religious life. Some believe the primary importance of community life is to witness to laity how people of diverse backgrounds can live together in Christian harmony. These insist that religious themselves are more important than the work they do: 'It's who we are as people, not what we do at work that is important,' claimed a forty-two-year-old sister. A fifty-year-old sister agreed: 'The focus should be more on the individual person's dedicated life. Where one lives and works is of less importance than what one is striving to become.' The majority, however, give first priority to ministry. A forty-year-old sister said: 'The reason for community, as far as I am concerned, is to strengthen us to carry out our service to the people.' And another sister in her thirties said:

Above everything else, religious are called to be change agents, to live on the prophetic edge. We're not that at the moment because, generally speaking, we are so involved with our communities, with maintaining the structures of the congregation and the institutional works that the energy for change is not there.

A few sisters separated ministry from work that provides financial support: 'Our ministry', remarked a sister in her early thirties, 'need not necessarily be our job.' Another, however, is making of whatever job she does her ministry. She works at present in a supermarket.

Underlying all speculations about the future of religious life is a frequently recurring belief in a new factor, the changes in relationship between religious and lay people. Religious are insisting that they are truly lay people and should be treated as such. As a thirty-nine-year-old sister said:

> There will be no élitism in the future. There will be no living on a pedestal wearing a starched collar or a big veil. Religious life will be very much inserted into the ordinary run of things: it will be very much part of ordinary human life. Hopefully, religious will be recognised as such by their attitudes and love of others, not by the rules they keep or the dress they wear.

Another sister, aged thirty-five, was very definite:

> If we are fair dinkum about bringing Jesus Christ to people or rather, helping people discover who this God is, then we must know their world as much as possible. We must know what their life is like. I see this as a very significant shift in attitude. Religious have to acknowledge they haven't answers: it's a case of religious and laity together searching for answers.

Such thinking leaves me with the impression that terms such as 'vow of poverty' and 'religious life', with their traditional connotations, may have to be discarded. For language can be an obstacle to the creation of new attitudes, thus preventing a vision from becoming enfleshed in reality. Although expressed in different terms, the fundamental principles of active religious life will endure — a deep personal relationship with God expressed in celibacy, and active membership of a group of similarly minded people who share resources in order to offer generous service to those in great need.

From this study one thing at least is obvious. If radical changes in present attitudes and values, with consequent implications for community and ministry, are not fully accepted and acted upon quickly, then deeply spiritual and creative religious women who are searching for ways to become more relevant in today's society — and for the support of like-minded, idealistic people — will either succumb to the weight of inertia and passivity within their congregations, or decide they can more effectively live and work for God outside religious life as they know it today. This study strongly indicates a choice is still possible, but the span of time for it is extremely short.